M000166668

6ix Kick-A$$ Strategies of the Million-Dollar Entrepreneur

Dawnna St Louis

DEDICATION

This book is dedicated to people who are crazy enough to think they can change the world. Here's your toolkit.
Go do it.

CONTENTS

v

ACKNOWLEDGMENTS

Thanks to the scrappy, crazy, stubbornly un-medicated business owners who work twenty-hour days for themselves so they don't have to work one minute for someone else. Here's to the middle-class mavericks who take big risks, garner big rewards, disrupt the status quo, and make magic happen even when no one believes. Thank you to the successful troublemakers, rebel rousers, and daredevils who recognize that the best part of sharing wealth is having someone to race your yacht against. Thank you to the naysayers that fuel my engine. Keep talking. My eternal love to the man who has supported my freedom to fly and believed that I could reach beyond the galaxy, even when my wing was broken. Here's to the woman who said just because *they* didn't, doesn't mean *you* can't - now go do it. I love you, mom. Thank you to the only things I've ever grown in my life – my sons - for making me laugh, cry, smile, think, and see things from a new perspective. Thank you to my friend for reminding me to work on my f*cking game and to stay mentally tough with a spicy dash of crazy. Here's to the man who crawls in my brain, pulls out the words, and helps me bring them to life. Here's to the woman who tailors these words and makes them make sense. Thanks to my right hand for keeping my left and life on point. And thanks to the reader who recognizes that words mean nothing without action. Read, learn, plan, do, and repeat these 6ix Kick-A$$ strategies and then report back on your struggles, your successes, your failures, and your millions!

ix

x

INTRODUCTION

This book will not suddenly transform you into a millionaire. Not today. Not tomorrow. Not ever. None of the information in this book comes from a higher power that will suddenly endow you with the sorcery required to pull a rabbit out of a hat. There is no magic here. To grow your business, you need to crack open a can of spinach, boost your courage, and run headfirst at the next giant hurdle like a dog with its tail on fire.

This book is an income building, busy-ness eradicating, get your sh*t together on a daily basis - business advice tool. Which is to say, it contains information that entrepreneurs have used to start, build, run, grow, and repeat their business success.

The trio of tools are the perfect trifecta needed to build a solid business foundation, spark strategic action towards business stability, and guidance for well-defined business improvement and continuous growth.

The first tool, The Business Blueprint, is just that - a blueprint. When you map your business to a simple twelve-point blueprint you get Superman level x-ray vision into those business blind spots that are killing your profit margin. Then there's The Daily 6ix, which delivers actionable strategies so you can prioritize what matters most every day – see eradicating busy-ness above. Finally, Kaizen, the last tool, provides insight into what works, what doesn't, and what you should do next to work smarter and not harder. In this, you can ultimately live the life and grow the business you deserve.

PART I
WHAT'S GOING ON

1

TICK-TOCK SLURP

Three months, two weeks, five days, seven hours, and forty-eight minutes. Forty-nine, fifty, fifty-one.

It was April, 2012 and my phone hadn't rung. There were no meetings on my calendar. There were no closed deals. Feeling desperate, I wanted an end to the slump. If I had five dollars, I would've paid a street-corner psychic to give me answers. Sure, they couldn't accurately predict the weather during a thunderstorm, but maybe they could tell me when my dry spell would end.

The silence in my office was maddening. I entertained myself by vociferously slurping hot java to the beat of the tick chasing the tock.

Tick - tock - tick-tickety - tock. Slurp.
Tick - tock - tick-tickety - tock. Slurp.
DING!

The sound of an incoming email interrupted my flow and sent me into action. This was the most excitement I'd seen in three months, two weeks, five days, seven hours, and fifty-two minutes. I sat straight and with a quick click of the mouse, the message came into full view.

"...I am contacting you in regards to a deceased client who died in an auto accident on the Madrid Highway in March. He was a prominent client of mine.
Before his death, my client and your wealthy Uncle deposited $22 million at the vault of a financial institution here in Africa."

All I had to do was send some personal information, along with my bank account numbers, and they would transfer the money within two business days. YAY UNCLE! I thought, as my fingers reflexively tapped the delete key. Now back to our regularly scheduled program. Tickety - tock. Slurp!

Those emails were a tempting mental distraction as time crawled by. What would happen if I sent them my info or my frenemies info? Would they deposit anything or would my bank account be as useless as it is right now? Do people really fall for this? I Googled *scam emails*.

My sales funnel was emptier than a pro-athlete's pockets after making it rain at a strip club. And my pipeline was no better. I could feel my business failing with every tick of that damned clock. Slurp!

Maybe I chose the wrong career path? My competitive mind would flash images of people who needed to be reminded to breathe on a regular basis, yet were making more money than me in the same industry. Maybe I should get a breathing machine—just in case. I Googled *breathing machines*.

To make matters worse, I had no real direction on what to do next. My professionally-suggested list of "supposed-to-dos" were all done.

I was *supposed* to have a great website, a memorable logo, and professionally photographed head-shots. I had all of that. I even hired a Vogue Magazine photographer and makeup artist to make me look like an untarnished, well-respected, trustworthy professional. They looked fantastic and convincing—like a stock photo you find on a bank's website. It looked nothing like me. Perfect.

I was *supposed* to have regular communications with my followers, so I made sure that Hootsuite™ app was making my perpetual social media presence felt.

I was *supposed* to have business cards that left a long-lasting impression, so I handed out snazzy high-end business cards like Halloween candy at networking events.

I was *supposed* to attend the monthly professional association meetings to keep up with the latest and greatest industry trends. I became a board member and soon discovered how much better everyone else claimed they were doing.

I did all the to-dos, except one: hire a business coach. There had to be someone out there who could give me a cure to funnel dryness that didn't involve squeezing KY™ jelly on in my pipeline.

Within a few minutes of checking with my professional social media group the referrals came in: Janice Crooner. She was *the one*! After a few light-weight vetting phone calls, I shelled out $4800 for a Midwestern encounter with "the pipeline profit-producing power player."

But thirty days after our initial call - short five grand and no new direction - I was back on the east coast of the US, slurping coffee to the tick-tickety - tock, yet again.

Janice had good information, but it wasn't anything I didn't already know, hadn't read on her website, or hadn't heard on her CD. There was no magic bullet from the Midwest. At the four month, three week, six day, ten hour, and thirty-one-minute mark my sales funnel was still drier than a stale bread and sandpaper sandwich.

I soon realized that following someone else's trampled trail leads to slim pickings and crappy leftovers.

It was time to get a horse, a torch, and blaze my own.

2

SELF-ANALYSIS

Like many second time business owners, I knew the entrepreneurial journey well. The highs were like 4/20 in Amsterdam and the lows were like a surprise drug test on 4/21. My history and experience gave me all the tools needed to start a business with just a telephone and good idea. Less than 20 years earlier my business partner, Allen, and I co-founded BizIntel, an international business intelligence company responsible for a team of careers, millions in revenue, and a 40% profit margin. My new business's projections were only a tenth of that with a much higher profit margin.

So, this new business venture should be about ten times easier, right?

Of course it should be easy. As long as easy means struggling like a 120-year-old stiletto-wearing stripper with a bum leg, pole-dancing for hip replacement money. Not only was I struggling, but the scrappy senior citizen was stealing my customers, my moves, and my tips!

It was time to have a come-to-Jesus meeting with the CEO in the mirror about this so-called business. Thus far, I proved myself to be just another business lemming blindly following the crowd, but no one was doing the same thing. So I wasn't sure what was working versus what wasn't or what I should do next.

The Mindset of an Entrepreneur

I was usually pretty good at making decisions, but for some reason picking a business model was kicking my ass. Was I selling to consumers or large corporations? Should I spend more time wooing consumers with great social media marketing campaigns or should I reach out to corporate decision makers who probably didn't spend a lot of their day on social media. My son, Travian, observed that because I struggled to make a decision likely meant I wasn't a serial killer and he was happy to finally check that off his list.

> Not really surprised that Travian had a list of concerns.
> I only wondered if he found my list about him and his brother.

It turns out that the Latin root of decide - *cide* - means "to kill." To decide an issue essentially means to kill the alternatives. Normally I was the Ted Bundy of alternative annihilation, but for some reason I was off my game.

Where had the entrepreneur gone that once started a new business with two sons in elementary school, a new house whose ink had barely dried on the page, and a husband working with a new company for only a few years. Where was the laser-focused woman who dared to take risks, reap rewards, and worry about the fall-out later. It was if someone had lobotomized her and left this indecisive wilderness wanderer feeling squeamish about the thought of eating grubs to survive.

She had to go and Dawnna 2.0 needed to emerge - fast. It wasn't about going back – I'd learned to much over the past twenty years to go back. It was about leveraging all the education, experience, tools, and courage (if I could muster it) at my disposal to move forward. To do so, I had to get my head right.

Queue JK Rowling.

As if divine intervention were paving a road to my future the story of JK Rowling, the author of the Harry Potter series, showed up as an article in my inbox. "Dawnna – seriously – read this now!" read the subject line.

The story goes that JK Rowling had tried to get agents to look at her book and she was turned down flat for over a year. When she finally did get a literary agent every publishing house turned her down. They hated the story,

9

her writing, the name Harry – it didn't matter – they hated everything. The rejection letters poured in like Moet on New Year's Eve in Paris.

This went on for another year until finally she was able to get an advance for four-thousand dollars from Bloomsbury. And the only reason she earned that much was due to Alice Newton, the eight-year-old daughter of Bloomsbury's chairman. She was given the first chapter to review by her father and immediately demanded the next. Ms. Rowling was told that while she continues writing the book, she should get off welfare and get a job to support her daughter as there was no money in children's books.

Today, JK Rowling is worth one billion dollars and the Harry Potter franchise is worth over fifteen billion.

JK's story got my juices flowing. I wondered what other rags-to-riches stories were out there. Maybe I just needed a little inspiration or a reminder of what it's like to be struggling entrepreneur who made it. My Google search coincidentally returned the story of two guys named Larry and Sergey.

When Larry and Sergey started their business in the garage of a college friend they were told that the search-engine market was saturated. No matter how many requests were made the dynamic duo couldn't get a meeting with investors. Today, Google isn't just their company's name, it's a verb.

Finally, I stumbled upon a story about Western Union. On an internal memo at Western Union it was written that "the telephone had entirely too many short-comings to be seriously considered as a viable means of communications".

Wow! I am like Pavlov's dog when it comes to answering my phone. Talking about not being able to see the possibilities.

These three stories taught me three very different lessons. JK Rowling's belief in herself propeller her even when other people literally told her that she wasn't good enough. Larry and Sergey didn't let an overcrowded marketplace stop them. In fact, if the marketplace is too crowded that means no one is standing out. There is an opportunity to be outstanding. And Western Union taught me that just because someone can't see your vision doesn't mean that you vision lacks merit.

I was inspired now I needed to take action.

The Problem with Decisions

Sensing that I was off my game, Travian suggested that I shouldn't choose a model, but rather draft two models. Regardless of which model I started with, I should give myself permission to choose again if one doesn't measure up.

I was ready to create my models and I knew exactly where to start. When Allen and I built BizIntel all those years ago, I kept a collection of little black diaries that detailed the six strategies we used to start, run, and repeat the success of business growth while sidestepping business landmines. All I had to do was climb into the crawlspace over the garage, evade cobwebs, anthrax, and Ebola, and dig through boxes to find them.

3

SINE QUA NON

What started as a class project, earning Allen top marks in his master's class and garnering much interest from the Dean of Entrepreneurship, turned out to be the source of our success when we started of BizIntel. The first four strategies were titled the Business Builder's Blueprint (B3), with The Daily 6ix and Kaizen strategies rounding out the last two. The Dean doted so much on the simplistic brilliance of the six business strategies that I thought Allen's over-inflated ego would need its own plaque. The Dean referred to it as the *sine qua non* of the project.

The Dean said, "Sine qua non means *without which not*. It means *that something* which is an essential part of the whole. Like a heart-beat is an essential part of life - the strategies shift focus to the essential components of business, removing distractions in the process. While it may be true that without good customer service, meetings, or communications you won't be in business for very long; the fact remains that without a business you won't have a need for any of these elements. Further, if there is inconsistency in your business, using these four strategies will reveal blind spots due to the heavy focus on the fundamentals."

This is exactly what my business needed. Even though I had all the puzzle pieces for a good business they were all to different puzzles. Something was missing and B3 was a perfect place to start. I knew it would take time and I had to have patience – currently in short supply. I also knew this one action would be the start of a positive change if I could just get it done.

B3 Overview

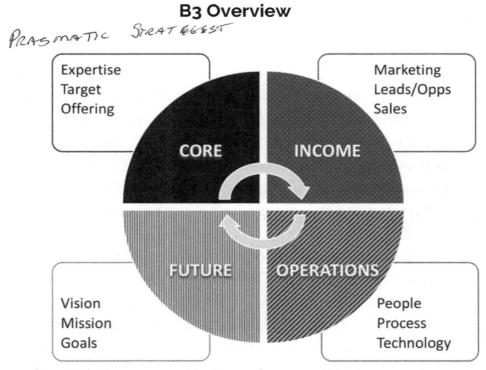

Figure 1 Business Builder's Blueprint

14

The B3 had four categorized strategies: Core, Income, Operations, and Future. The top half of the B3 pie (Core and Income) is all about profits, while the bottom half (Operations and Future) is all about running a business. Starting with the Core, a business owner would head clockwise through each quadrant until their business is completely mapped. Any areas causing significant difficulty are likely to be a blind spot or have a blind spot directly before or after it.

Let's say that your business is having trouble with leads. There is usually one of two issues causing the problem: either the leads are not right for the business or the business can't convert a lead to a sale.

If you can't convert a lead to a sale then your sales strategies and tactics, pricing, sales teams, etc., need an overhaul. But if the issues are with the quality of the lead then your marketing needs some work. If your marketing is the problem, then we'd work backwards through the Core Strategy to figure out what's going wrong.

I was ready to dip my toes into this pool of strategies. While I knew they worked I was concerned with how long it would take and how much of what I already built would be thrown away. But in my soul I knew that if I wanted to build a new empire that I needed a solid foundation. And the B3 would deliver exactly that.

PART II
THE BUSINESS BUILDERS BLUEPRINT

4

STRATEGY 1:
STRENGTHEN YOUR CORE

When GEICO opened its doors in 1936 they provided auto insurance to government employees. The founder, Leo Goodwin, had previously worked for USAA, an insurer which only provided insurance for military personnel. Goodwin predicated his model on the USAA model and targeted only government employees. He thought that government employees, as a group, would constitute a less risky and more financially stable pool of customers. In fact, the name of the company is an acronym: Government Employees Insurance Company.

> GEICO still keeps their target customers very exclusive with extremely high standards in underwriting.

Today, GEICO's offerings are significantly different. Over the years they've diversified and now offer home, auto, boat, and motorcycle insurance to the public. Goodwin increased his chances of success by keeping his target small and his offering specific. GEICO is a prime example of a company that maintained a strong core and then diversified by leveraging that core from the very beginning.

Core Strategy

Lower back pain, poor posture, bad balance, and that nasty hangover you get after gorging a full box Oreos are all telltale signs of a weak core. My personal fitness trainer made this abundantly clear when he used me as the "before" person in his before/after example.

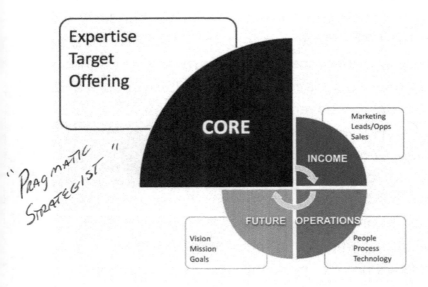

Figure 2 Core Strategy Quadrant

The same is true of any business. If the core is weak then you'll be broke, busy, frustrated, and indecisive. My business was suffering from all of these - low income, overloaded operations, ineffective marketing, and crappy decision-making.

The Core Strategy defines the organization's expertise, the target market, and the offerings used to deliver that expertise to the target market. The core of my business needed strengthening if it was going to be ready for bikini season – or at least a cover-up to wear over the bikini.

Your Expertise

The first step was to define my expertise. Not to brag here, but like everyone else with an IQ above 50, I thought I had too much expertise to choose from. How could I pick just one? I was a certified project management professional (PMP), Six Sigma Black Belt, excellent trainer, keynote speaker, I'd built and sold a successful company, I could tie my shoes with one hand, and belt out an amazing tune in the shower. Obviously, I knew enough to fill up at least one Wikipedia page. The task of finding my expertise would be easier if I had less brilliance to offer the world. I Googled *the benefits of a lobotomy.*

The Five Focus Factor Questions – Be, Know, Do, Have, Solved - were key to discovering my expertise:
- What have I been (significant role) that others would want to do or would benefit from doing

the same? *Successful Sales / Consultant.*

With the answer the first question in mind, answer the remaining questions:

- What have I done that others would like to do or would benefit from doing? *15 year visiting more than 500 dealerships*
- What do I know that others would benefit from knowing? *insight from personal experience How to become successful in Sales*
- What do I have that others would benefit from having? *Experience*
- With the answers to the above questions in mind, what challenge do I solve? *moving you from Here to there*

I pondered these questions and came up with the perfect answer - followed by a new answer the next day and a different answer on the third. By the end of the week I was back at the first answer sprinkled with elements of the second and third answer. Remember when I said, "If your core is weak then decision making will suffer." Yeah...that was happening. I couldn't decide which area of my expertise was *the* expertise. When I couldn't choose I blended them all into some kind of hodge-podge expertise that no one ever heard of.

Since I obviously had too much to offer and was too smart to answer these questions (not!), I looked for patterns in the answers of other companies and C-Level executives.

- Leo Goodwin
  - Role (Be): Insurance Executive

22

- o Know: Detailed knowledge and inner-working on the insurance industry
- o Do: How to build an insurance company for a specific market
- o Have: The investment money, contacts, and marketing chops to create a niche market in insurance
- o Solve: For the customer – lower cost insurance without low cost service. For his business - The challenge of keeping long-term customers in the insurance industry.
- Broward County Water Utilities
  - o Role (Be): Deliverer of clean water to farmers
  - o Know: How to deliver clean water
  - o Do: Obtain and deliver clean water; set up the infrastructure; manage water delivery, etc.
  - o Have: Start-up infrastructure to deliver clean water
  - o Solve: The delivery of clean water to those without it.
- BMW
  - o Role (Be): Engineers of jet engines
  - o Know: The secrets of creating the ultimate flying machine (hmmmm.... Transferrable knowledge?)
  - o Do: Build high performance aircraft
  - o Have: The engineers, warehouses, and

machinery required to build performance aircraft. Relationships with automotive builders. A reputation for building airplanes
- o Solve: A gap in the market for those desiring jet-performance in a vehicle.

Initially, I thought the redundancy in answers meant that I didn't understand the three questions. Turns out, it was less about redundancy and really focusing on the core. When I looked back at my business intelligence company, I saw that we were focused on *business intelligence that helped our clients predict the future*, and all signs pointed to that expertise repeatedly. Sure, we had project management and application development departments, but they only existed to *deliver business intelligence solutions*.

I tested B3 with my friend Christian who had a thriving business. He was always busy traveling from one conference to another, closing deals, and diversifying his offering. I was sure that his core would be succinct and his responses redundant. I was wrong again.

"Leadership coaching, presentation skills, customer service excellence, sales training, and holistic medicine," he listed off as his expertise.

"I didn't know your business was so...uh...diversified," I said.

Christian replied, "Yes, and it's killing me! My marketing is all over the place. I have five different websites. Eight different mailing lists. Sometimes I run a B2B model. Other times I run a B2C model. I'm busy all the time. My profit margin sucks and all I want to do is teach executives how to leverage mindfulness for better business success."

I wondered if he knew how ironic it was that mindfulness wasn't on his list or that he wasn't practicing it in his business.

Just like a runner can't win a race by running in every lane, Christian couldn't win in business being pretty good at everything. He was trying to be known for everything. Instead he was known for nothing.

To increase the commas in my bank account I knew I had to decrease the commas in my expertise. My expertise is the sine qua non of my Core Strategy and the Rosetta stone of my business structure. Without it, the B3 and the rest of the strategies would crumble.

Your Target Market

The term target market always brings to mind images of me dressed up like Robin Hood holding a bow and arrow, hunting down my prey in the Sherwood Forest. In one clean shot I'd bring back my winnings! However, in reality, I started as a novice archer. I worried: how long do I have to wait for my prey? Would they be kicking and screaming or would they come along willingly? Do I use duct tape to tie them up? What's the best arrow to use? The whole thing felt exhausting!

What I loved about GEICO's start in business was that Goodwin looked at an entire market and created an offering that only one segment of the population couldn't resist. My mother had GEICO auto insurance for years. Their rates were very competitive and the service was fantastic. I remember my Aunt Lila complaining that she couldn't get GEICO no matter how hard she tried. GEICO created more than a target market, they created desirability of which only a privileged few could take advantage. GEICO still has very high underwriting standards. It's like a private club.

Instead of thinking of a target market as the people I would go after, I needed to think of them as a clamoring horde who would go after me. From this eager crowd I would select specific individuals for entry into my private club. They would be required to meet distinct criteria to be afforded the privilege of my expertise. That sounded way better than wearing green tights in the woods.

After speaking to several of my colleagues, I soon discovered that the everybody-wants-me bandwagon was pretty full of people like Christian.

My colleague Elena is a Latina who believes deeply in women's empowerment and women-owned businesses.

When I asked her about the perfect target audience for her business branding services she said, "Everyone". I found the answer incredulous and questioned further.

"Really? Every one of the seven billion inhabitants of planet Earth wants your business branding services. Really?"

Elena thought my question was as silly as I thought her answer was. She then told me that everyone could use her services and she doesn't want to turn anyone away. Still not satisfied with her answers I pressed. "So the Grand Dragon of the KKK (a violent white supremacist group) wants to ramp up their domestic abuse campaign. They really feel like the wives who don't agree with their doctrine are getting out of hand. They think your business branding services would be helpful for the new spinoff brand K3W2 or Klu Klux Klan Wife Whackers. Are you taking them on as a client?"

Elena was taken aback. "Of course not Dawnna! What a stupid question." I reminded her that she didn't want to turn anyone away.

Elena wasn't the only one. Colleague after colleague talked about being the right choice for everyone or that they could share their expertise and offering with everyone. But the question isn't *who could use your offering*, the question is *who you be proud to call a member of your private club that would value your offerings the most?*

27

I was sure that Elena would be embarrassed if the KKK said that her services were fantastic. After a deeper conversation Elena admitted that she was concerned that if she niched or focused on a target market that she would miss out on business.

She wasn't alone. I had the same struggle. I was concerned with what I would miss out on if I selected a target market.

This issue was plaguing me. I knew the right answer was to create a tightly focused target market, but I was also afraid of missing out on business. During a conversation with my mom she shared this story:

Imagine that you are out having lunch with your coworker, Bob, when a total stranger walks up to you and gives you one million dollars. Then the stranger turns to Bob and gives him five million dollars. And before walking away, the stranger says, "Have a better day."

Bob just got four million dollars more than you. What do you say? How do you feel?

Initially I asked questions like: Why did Bob get five million dollars? What makes him so special? Why did I get ripped off? So focused on the fact that Bob got five million dollars, I missed out on the free and clear million-dollar stash sitting in my lap.

My mom continued, "Your target market is a free stash of cash. Don't worry about Bob's five million dollars. You can't spend it anyway and it doesn't impact you. You know you can't win a race running in every lane but you also can't win by picking a lane and then focusing on several finish lines. Pick a target and go for it."

My good friend, John, is a ghostwriter and writing coach who, like me, used to be concerned with Bob's five million until he saw the light.

John worked with anyone who wanted a book written. It didn't matter whether it was about giant feet on small women in China, waterfront real estate deals in the Arctic Circle, or the secret and salacious lives of naked bungee jumpers. His target market was anyone, anywhere, anytime. He didn't want to miss out on opportunities - even if the opportunity wasn't right for him.

John's skills weren't recognized in any specific market and, to make matters worse, he wasn't targeting business as much as he was waiting for business to land on his doorstep.

When his business went through a particularly long famine period, John knew things had to change. He could no longer only react to the market, he had to make strides to own it.

John looked over the span of his career to find where he could best leverage his writing expertise. He'd started writing for magazines about wine, subsequently completing two books on the subject. Not only was John passionate about wine, he was well-versed on the subject, so he began working with wineries. He worked as a ghostwriter composing the long and storied histories of vineyards. The response was large and instantaneous. He had found his target market and his target market was excited to have him.

John Lydgate said it best, "You can please some of the people all of the time, you can please all of the people some of the time, but you can't please all of the people all of the time".

When John and Goodwin both selected target markets that were in line with their past experiences, they found a target market waiting for them – one that would be easy to please all the time. I knew that the best place to find my target market was in my history.

Your Offering

The scribble in the corner of the diary read: "How do they want it? What are they willing to pay for it?"

They were my target market and *it* was my expertise - that much was clear. What wasn't clear was the offering. I needed to decide how my target market wanted to access my expertise, when and how often they wanted to access it, and what premium services would they find valuable over time. Fortunately, the Cost/Access Ladder would provide great insight.

The Cost/Access Ladder (Figure 3) shows the transition of a customer from a free interested browser to a premium customer with private access. The left side of the diagram indicates the cost, while the right side indicates access. The higher level, privileged, or private access would garner highest or premium cost.

Using a typical airline company as an example, we can see how the customer pays more for higher levels of service and access.

Figure 3 Cost / Access Ladder

When you first initiate interest or purchase, the cost is free for customer service and online reservation access. The airline uses its website to transform a marketing opportunity into a strong sales lead. In many cases, if a customer starts to reserve a seat and does not complete the reservation, the airline will send a follow-up email in an effort to close the sale.

For a small fee, some airlines offer a subscription to deals and upgrades. For example, if a customer signs up for the airline's emails, the customer will get a free checked bag or access to special deals. The cost, in this case, is the customer's information while the access is early access to premium deals.

Customers can further upgrade and enjoy early boarding and priority service or larger seats in business class. If a customer is loyal to the airline and has accumulated a predetermined number of miles or paid for first class, they will enjoy the highest level of seating, service, and lounge access. This access, however, is limited to very few who've paid for the privilege.

I felt prepared to work on my Core Strategy. And after four months, three weeks, two days, eighteen hours, and nineteen minutes into a sales drought that didn't have an end in sight - I nailed it!

The core of my business finally had the kind of clarity

that I needed to move forward. I knew for the first time ever exactly what I sold, to whom I sold it, and how I delivered it. Now I was ready to make some real profits.

5

STRATEGY 2:
INCREASE YOUR INCOME

No one gives two coitus cats in cake-covered kitty-litter about what you sell. No one. Not even your mother. Unless you're selling Girl Scout cookies - everyone likes Girl Scout cookies. Otherwise, people simply care that you can solve their problem when they need you to solve it. And only in a way that makes them better off.

Let's say that you want to buy a drill. Will it be a Dewalt? Bosch? Milwaukee? Before you can answer that question, you need to know why you need it. What problem will your drill solve? If you're using the drill to put a hole in something, then any of the above drills should work just fine. But what if you were doing some decorative staging for a home's garage and you need a drill to match the red, black, and white decor? Then a red Milwaukee would suit your needs better than Dewalt's yellow exterior or Bosch's blue hue. The Milwaukee delivers a solution the other drills don't - it matches your decor.

I don't buy coffee. I buy a remedy that transforms me into a socially functional human being.

The solution that you sell is more important than the product. Now let's turn that solution into profits!

Most people would say that if you aren't making money you have a hobby - not a business. I would go a little further and say that you don't have a business until you can draw a trend line to future revenues. Until then, you are a contractor working to fulfill one contract after another – a lesson taught to me by a surly accountant.

When Allen and I inked our first BizIntel contract we did what most entrepreneurs do. We gave ourselves lofty titles, purchased flamboyant business cards, and hired a good accountant to keep us out of an IRS established penitentiary. Then we did the work of the contract. Roughly twelve months into a twenty-four-month contract, we thought we should get another contract before our first contract ran out. We were both pretty passionate about not starving.

In our minds we were business owners. It wasn't until our accountant said, "A business is defined by your intention to make money. Since you can't show a trend of intent, you are not business owners - you're contractors."

I took umbrage. "But we have titles and look at our business cards."

"Those are nice. Show me what your future earnings will look like over the next five years and I will call you a business. Show me how your marketing efforts lead to new opportunities. Show me how those opportunities turn into sales. You are predictive model gurus - you literally can predict the future for everyone except yourself. Until you can quantifiably show me that you have a future, you're contractors, not business owners." And with that he slammed shut his black leather briefcase and left us standing dumbfounded - flamboyant business cards and all.

The accountant was right. Our core was strong, but we weren't creating future revenues for our business.

It was almost twenty years later and those words were echoing through time. I knew that if I wanted to avoid business famine again then I had to get a grip on continuous income production.

Income Strategy

The Income Strategy, if worked properly, will stave off starvation. It determines how an organization communicates offerings to its target market (marketing), how those communications translate into opportunities (leads), and how those opportunities become income (sales). The Income Strategy ensures that you make money intentionally.

Figure 4 Income Strategy Quadrant

Just like sit-ups leverage your core to transform your belly into six-pack abs, the Income Strategy leverages your Core Strategy by translating your expertise into profits and giving insight into your pitfalls when things get lost in translation.

I was going to write planks instead of sit-ups. But I am pretty sure that planks are God's way of telling us to stop working out.

Your Marketing

If ever there was a black hole of money and time wasted in business it is marketing. Marketers may say that they can't give you a quantifiable Return On Investment (ROI) percentage because, blah, blah, blah. All that matters is that you cough up five kajillion dollars for an entry level social media package that guarantees nothing. You know you need marketing, but you don't know how to do it, so you negotiate three kajillions, a kidney, and naming rights to your first born.

Whoa! Back away from the checkbook! Marketing is critical. And yes - you must do it by testing, measuring, and determining how to improve. But make sure you have a strategy first, then figure out if one of those social media mavericks can help you do it. Whether you hire a good marketing company to execute based on your strategy or whether you get smart, like Chris Dingman of the Dingman Group, it needs to be a priority. Chris Dingman relocates athletes worldwide and is proud to say that he has a zero-dollar marketing budget. Chris leverages relationships for marketing - no money required for a handshake.

To create a decent marketing strategy, you need to understand what problems you solve, why your target market wants your solution from a logical and emotional perspective, and how much value they put on your solution.

OFFER A PRACTICAL, LOGICAL SOLUTION OR PROCESS TO MOVE YOU FORWARD. FROM WHERE YOU ARE RIGHT NOW,

Logical Justification

The primary point of marketing is not to sell a product but rather, to offer a solution. It's up to your marketing team to convey a solution in such a way that your target market will feel compelled to move into action.

People aren't normally compelled to buy based on logic, however, logic gives your target market a business case to justify the purchase. The two quantifiable justifications that cause people to buy are: *the reduction of pain and the increase of pleasure*. Both can be summed up into four categories:

- Time:
  - Too much time wasted is bad
  - Extra time and higher efficiency is good
- Work
  - Too much work or hard work is bad
  - Easy work and high productivity is good
- Money
  - High debt, empty pockets, no money is bad
  - Lots of money, fat pockets, no debt is good
- Quality
  - Unhealthy, unhappy, afraid, worse, less is bad
  - Healthy, happy, better, easier, more is good

Regardless which of the first three you choose; they mean nothing if quality isn't increased. Quality is always required.

Let's suppose that you work for a moving company. The owner is excited because the new fleet of trucks have shiny red side-loading doors. As far as you can tell these new doors save you no time, they don't make your work easier, and you won't save or earn any money. They are simply shiny red doors.

But what if I told you that the doors will make it easier for you to load and unload faster because they open wider and increase headroom? This will save you time and likely help you garner bigger tips due to extra speedy service. Now those doors sound pretty amazing - don't they?

An improvement of time, work, or money, and quality is the solution that your customer is buying, not the shiny red side-loading doors. When determining the solution you provide, it is critical to define the business case or the logical justification for the purchase; but not before you get buy-in from their emotions.

Emotional Justification

Once you understand your target market's justification for your offering, you need to understand emotionally why they want it. Emotional triggers are very powerful and often outweigh logic. This list of emotional triggers, followed by logical ones, is used every day by big advertising companies:

- Pride:
  - o I want to feel like I am better than everyone else. I want everyone to know I am the best. I want to be proud of...
- Envy:
  - o I want what they have.
- Greed:
  - o I feel like I should have everything I desire. I want to feel like I got the deal of the century. I want everyone to know how much I have and that I have a lot.
- Lust:
  - o I want to be sexy and desired. I want everyone to see how amazing I am. I want to be seen and known. I want people to lust after me. I want others to rely on me and need me.
- Wrath:
  - o I want to annihilate the competition. I want them to know that I won. I want everyone to bow to my greatness.
- Gluttony:
  - o I want more than I need or could even imagine having.
- Sloth:
  - o I want everything to be easier, better, and faster so I can do or have more with less exertion.

If that list of seven words looks familiar, it should. They are the Seven Deadly Sins. And advertisements tantalize our most sinful desires to get us emotionally charged and then connect with logic so that we can justify the purchase. They know that if you're emotionally charged enough, then logic will take a back seat in your decision-making process. People buy first with their heart and then with their head.

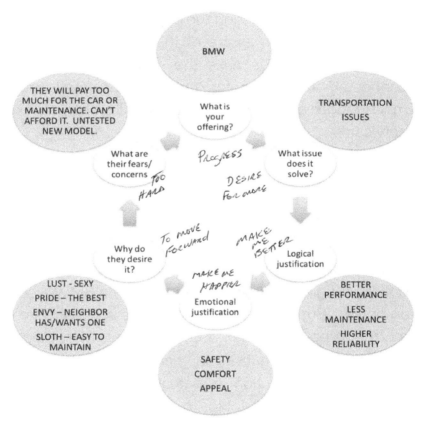

Figure 5 Understanding the desires of your target market

Think about the last time you saw a commercial about the latest model BMW on the road. You might have heard words like *sexy*, *exciting*, and *reliable* which translates into lust, lust, and a little bit of pride. You probably saw a woman with long tan legs getting into a car followed by a handsome gentleman closing her door. BMW emotionally connected with you before telling you the cost.

Logically, you would never purchase a new automobile - it's a poor investment. Cars lose their value the moment they leave the assembly line. And that value continues to plummet even as you sign the paperwork. Every consumer purchasing a car is aware of this, and yet the purchase happens anyway because the consumer is emotionally connected with the color, the new car smell, and how much longer and tanner their legs will look in an exciting new car.

The emotional connection of the BMW to the viewer is undeniable. If BMW advertisers have done their job, many viewers will desire that car. The logical connection, however, ensures that only the target market they are trying to reach gets it. If the viewer has sixty thousand dollars hanging around, then they know a BMW 4 series is an option. But if sixty thousand dollars sounds more like a mortgage payment than a car payment, then the viewer will consider alternatives in their price point. While the emotional connection creates inclusivity and gets everyone interested, logic (the price) creates exclusivity and cuts away those who can't afford it.

It is BMW's way of assuring that only those who can afford it make an effort to enter their private club.

Understand Your Value

Two of the most valuable pricing lessons I learned in business had to do with a Ferrari. It changed how I looked at doing my business with people and how I priced my offering.

Lesson #1:

Answer the following question:
Would you buy a $240K Ferrari for $20K?
This is all the information you need.
Now what is your answer? Yes, or no?

There are two ways to answer this question.
A. No. There is something wrong with the Ferrari.
B. Yes. The seller is either desperate or an idiot, but I'm getting a deal.

If you answered A you recognize that when a deal is too good to be true it probably is and you walk away. If you answered B, then you think that the seller is stupid and you have likely underestimated the person on the other side of the business deal.

Underestimating who you're doing business with is the second biggest mistake in business.

Lesson #2:

You just purchased a $240K Ferrari for $240K. Yeah, no deals here. After six months of Nascar level in-town driving, you need to get some brakes. You get two estimates.

Jethro's Service Shop is pretty sure that brakes are brakes and a Ferrari is no different from a Ford. Jethro's estimate is $250. You get the second estimate from a certified Ferrari mechanic, who tells you that just the front set of brakes costs over $550. He estimates that it will run you $1250, including labor.

When you are pushing the limits on that next curve and really need your brakes to perform at the highest possible level, who do you trust to perform the work:

A. Jethro at $250
B. Certified Ferrari Mechanic at $1250

Most people, who prefer not to eat their food through a straw for the rest of their lives, would choose B. The reasons are clear - they want to know that they'll be safe and secure. A certified mechanic charging a reasonable rate gives you the confidence you need to press the brake pedal at 150 miles per hour.

This is the first lesson in pricing: never underestimate (and in rare cases overestimate) your value. Many times organizations price themselves as Jethro and then wonder why they have limited business. If it's too cheap, something is wrong with it. Jethro might be a fantastic mechanic, but if he can't see his value, then why should his customer?

When Marketing Works - Really Works

When the solutions defined in your marketing relieves their frustrations you get results like that of the Dollar Shave Club (DSC).

Figure 6 Frustrations Analysis Diagram for Dollar Shave Club

Dollar Shave Club was founded by Mark Levine and Michael Dubin. The pair met at a party and spoke of their frustrations with the cost and challenge of buying razor blades. With their own money and investments from start-up incubator Science Inc., they began operations in July 2011.

On March 6, 2012, the company uploaded a YouTube

47

video entitled "Our Blades Are F***ing Great" featuring CEO Michael Dubin. The video prompted 12,000 orders in a two-day span after it was released, and as of March 2016 has received over 22 million views.

We can map DSC's connection to the customer using the Frustrations Analysis Diagram (FAD). DSC solved the fear and frustration associated with buying blades. They tapped into the negative emotions the buyer was feeling and gave them a positive alternative. As a result, Dollar Shave Club delivers sixteen blades to a subscriber's door for nine dollars a month. While that seems like a huge discount, it's only a savings of about one dollar per week.

Leads and Sales

Great leads are a direct result of great marketing. If your marketing is great and your leads are great, then sales should be easier. If you're still struggling with sales, then take a closer look at the quality of your sales team, pricing, and sales process.

Figure 7 Good Marketing Results

Poor marketing causes poor leads, which causes you and your sales team to work overtime to make a sale. If you hate your leads, take a closer look at your Marketing Strategy and potentially, your Core Strategy.

Figure 8 Poor Marketing Results

In 1997, the Taco Bell Chihuahua was the fast-food chain's big attempt to establish a mascot for their brand. And while everyone was quoting the dog's *Yo quiero Taco Bell* catch-phrase, the ads were directly linked to a 6 percent drop in Taco Bell sales. Competitors claimed that Taco Bell was advertising that their food was a dish only a dog would eat.

But if you look closer, the dog and its catchphrase were gimmicks that didn't connect with the buyer emotionally. This poor marketing strategy led to a decline in sales.

Edu-Sales

Ken's Krafts designs unique corporate gifts from sustainably sourced wood. His target market consists of salespeople or executives who want to give interesting gifts - something other than run-of-the-mill. His clients have higher than average budgets and are looking for fewer than five hundred pieces. When Ken's Krafts cultivates a lead that meets the company's criteria, the only thing he needs to do is educate his buyer.

Ken can then talk about the quality of his work, turnaround times, design specialty, other services, and the added bonus of delivering a story about the source of the wood. But Ken never has to convince his target market that his product is for them or that they need to deliver unique gifts. They already know this. And for Ken, understanding the nuance between convince and convey allows him to make speedy, selective decisions about which leads to pursue.

The Indecisive: I like it but... Maybe we need a committee. I could go either way.

The Learner: I want to know a bit about everything. I'll tell everyone.

The Avoider: Send me some literature that I can throw away.

The Runner: Everything new is a risk. Go away!

The Daredevil: I want to show everyone that I got it first!

More convincing. Lower Sales.　　More Conveying. Higher Sales.

Figure 9 Prime Customer Curve

Take a look at the Customer Curve above. The Runner, The Avoider, and The Indecisive all have to be convinced that your solution is the right solution. But The Learner and The Daredevil are already interested. They want to be educated to understand how your solution specifically solves their issue.

The secret sauce to sales has little to do with your history or your product, but relies on how well you educate your buyer. If they knew what you knew about your offering, would they buy? If the answer is no, then you need to change your line of work.

I followed Chris Dingman's path and learned just enough about marketing to be dangerous. By creating enticing campaigns for my target market, my sales funnel delivered a stream that ended my income drought. I had a long way to go but after six months, two weeks, three days, eleven hours, and thirteen minutes, it felt good be heading in the right direction.

6

STRATEGY 3:
OPTIMIZE YOUR OPERATION

When I'd head out the door with the type of friends that my mother didn't care for she'd say, "You are judged by the company you keep, the actions you take, and the tools you use. A hard head can be used to drive a nail but only a fool would do it; and their stupid friends would let them." Her words followed me throughout business. Little did I know that my mother had planted the seeds of people, process, and technology - a strategy that would follow me for the rest of my professional life.

People, Process, and Technology (PPT) first formally made its way into my career when I became a Six Sigma Black Belt. I recognized that to optimize anything, PPT was required. After starting my business intelligence company, this same trio popped up again as the core of successful holistic implementation. And finally working as a deep tech geek, PPT was the baseline upon which every successful technology project was judged.

It only made sense that the sine qua non of an optimized operations strategy would leverage People, Process, and Technology.

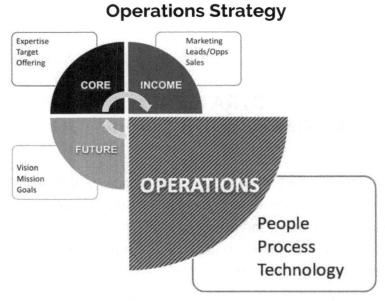

Figure 10 Operations Strategy Quadrant

Doing the same thing over and over again and expecting different results may be the definition of insanity, but if you want to go insane in business, keep reinventing the wheel. Your Operations Strategy is where you keep your business sanity when things go nuts. This is where you bring together the people who are paramount to the success of your organization, the processes used to reach common goals, and the technology leveraged to optimize work.

People, Process, and Technology (PPT)

The first time I saw a PPT diagram in my entrepreneurial role I thought, "Well hell, there's the problem. I have no people. Let me go grab some from the local Dollar Store." But my experience taught me better. Even solopreneurs have people - it's the solopreneur. While I was tempted to start my Operations Strategy with People, I realized that Process is actually the best starting point.

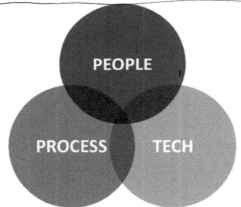

Figure 11 People, Process, and Technology Diagram

Processes are repetitive actions that people and/or technology execute to reach a specific goal. Consider ordering a drink at Starbucks.

- You place your order for a drink
- The cashier scribbles your name and the specification of your order on a cup
- Places your cup in line behind other cups
- You pay for your order
- The barista prepares your drink based on the specs

- Your name is called and your drink is placed on the counter for your retrieval

Seems pretty simple and runs like a well-oiled wrestler down a slip-n-slide. Though, imagine for a moment that a single barista handled all the steps alone during the 8am rush. That barista would be woefully overloaded and fail miserably. But this is what so many new entrepreneurs, new leaders, and small business owners do. They believe that they must singularly own every part of the process and that no one can do any part of the process as well as they can.

Recognizing and correcting this mistake is where people and technology come into play. Not only do you want to hire the right people, you also want to leverage technology to optimize the process of managing and reaching your goals.

People and Process

You can't throw nine women at a pregnancy and have a baby in a month. You need to know what you're doing before you add more people to help do it. And that is why the first P in PPT should be process and not people.

Think of processes as the stuff you do every day, how quickly you do it, the order in which you get it done, and the dependencies of that action. In the Starbucks example, the barista making coffee is dependent on the customer placing an order. The speed at which the coffee is made is dependent upon swiftness of the steamer heating up the coffee, the briskness of the cashier's scribbles, and the agility of the barista to get the job done. All of these actions play a part in the duration of the process.

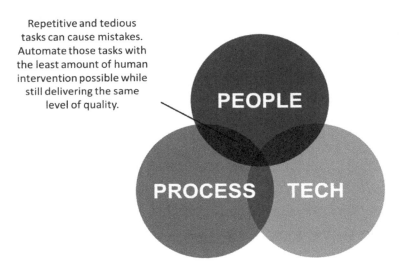

Repetitive and tedious tasks can cause mistakes. Automate those tasks with the least amount of human intervention possible while still delivering the same level of quality.

Figure 12 People and Process Diagram

When defining a process, you need to first understand the goal and then tweak elements for improvement. For Starbucks, the goal is to provide the customer the coffee they ordered as quickly as possible. If doing something faster leads to poorer results, then reduce the speed. Yep - going slower is a valid solution.

At an airport in Texas customers complained that they waited twice as long to retrieve their bags at baggage claim than in most airports. Process improvement gurus measured the task of getting luggage from an airplane to baggage claim faster and simply could not find a way to streamline the process without major and costly construction. Therefore, instead of speeding up the luggage to baggage claim, they slowed down the passengers by making the route to baggage claim longer. The airport now boasts high customer service ratings in the baggage claim department.

Once you understand and document each of your processes then you can start thinking about the people required to complete them.

If you are a recovering control freak entrepreneur, like I am, then it is difficult to let go and hand off to other people. But, I also knew that if I wanted to grow my business I couldn't do everything. To relinquish control and still remain sane this step-by-step process made it easier.

- Create a list of all the processes that you do in a single month. It is easier to do take a full month to do this than to try and create the list in one sitting.
- Score each activity 1-10 in regards to how well you do the work. The higher proficiency earns the higher score.
- Go back through each activity and add the following letter designation for each:
  - A – I should be doing it
  - B – I should not be doing it

- Plot each item to the Business Activities Delegation Table to determine the proper action to take.

	A	B
10 9 8 7 6	Do these activities	Teach these activities
5 4 3 2 1	Learn these activities	Hire for these activities

Table 1 Business Activities Delegation Table

By plotting your activities in the Business Activities Delegation Table you will gain a clear view into where you are spending your time, where you should be spending your time and those activities to delegate.

When I followed this diagram, it was easier than I thought to delegate the *hire for these activities* items. I wasn't good at the activities, I didn't like doing them, and would spend no time micromanaging them. My new team member knew that I all wanted was results. I left it up to her to determine how I would get them.

People and Technology

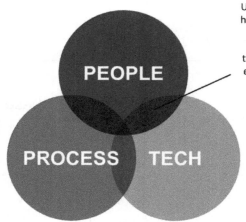

Use technology to enhance how you work with people. Phones, text messaging, email, and Skype all use technology to create more efficient communications. Use only as needed.

Figure 13 People and Technology

You can use a carrier pigeon or smoke signal to get a message to your client. It might not be the best way to communicate and your clients might leave you, but there are no rules here.

Getting quality work done more efficiently is where technology comes into play. Even while writing this book, it was easier to collaborate with my writing coach and editor using Google Docs than it was to save a document, manage different versions, and emailing versions back and forth.

But technology is often confused with the zeros and ones associated with computers. Tiger Woods took the golfing world by storm in 1996, at the age of 20, when he won two tournaments in his first season on the PGA tour. In 1997 he won four tournaments and became the youngest golfer to win the Masters. I am fairly certain that he would not have done so well using a hockey stick. Sometimes the technology you need is found in the tool you use.

Technology and Process

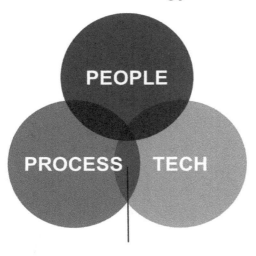

Email marketing campaigns, morning coffee, and online sales all use process and technology with minimal human intervention

At 7am my Keurig coffee maker steams out my first caramel macchiato, transforming me from an anti-social hydra into a somewhat socially acceptable human being. At 2pm my Roomba robot leaves its dock, sweeps my floor, and freaks out my dog. And every hour on the hour, until it's full, my freezer makes the ice I use for afternoon margaritas and daiquiris. Without the technology automatically running these processes I might actually have to do them myself. Imagine the horror.

All three activities require minimal human intervention and are the definition of automation. They support the process and eliminate tedious and repetitive tasks. In business we see this type of automation with Customer Relationship Management (CRM) campaigns, auto-responders for emails, and calendar reminders for appointments.

> The elimination of people in the Technology and Process relationship would lead to the rise of the machines. That's a whole other book and blockbuster movie. See I, Robot as a reference.

Technology and Process do not eliminate the participation of People, but rather minimizes how often people are involved in the process.

Define Your Own PPT

Jamie Chambers, a colleague and productivity expert, complained that her day was overrun with random tasks. She had to forage for leads, put the leads in her CRM, execute her sales strategy including follow-ups, and then deliver on the contracts she'd already sold. Many times she stopped her sales process in order to deliver the services that she'd already sold, which threw her business into famine. Then she'd restart her sales process when the contracts ran out in hopes of returning to feast mode.

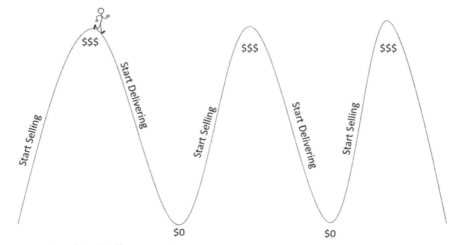

Figure 14 Jamie's Rollercoaster

Jamie finally jumped off this crazy rollercoaster by following a straightforward strategy used by Six Sigma experts who specialize in process improvement.

Step 1: Define Your Processes

Over several weeks Jamie listed all of the actions executed in her business. Here is a high level view of her list:

- Gather new leads
- Upload, tag, and categorize new leads into CRM
- Add leads into email campaign based on tag/category
- Reach out to interested opportunities
- Write new agreements
- Collections
- Create new client packet
- Lead client coaching

63

- Follow up with clients

Although Jamie's list is significantly longer than what is shown here, from a high level we can see several activities that could easily be outsourced. But before Jamie heads down the path of outsourcing activities, she needs to get a handle on what actually transpires during each activity and its duration. This information will be valuable when hiring someone to handle the work.

Step 2: Measure Your Processes

Jamie wrote out all parts of each process. She identified the steps, their duration, the tools and technology used, the responsible parties, and all the dependencies. While this was a lot of work, it was a critical step in understanding where and how she could streamline her process.

Step 3: Analyze Your Processes

I remember walking into Jamie's conference room - now jokingly dubbed The Room of Lost Trees - and took in the expanse of the scene. Every wall was covered with papers documenting one process after another. "No wonder I'm tired and broke. Only three of these processes actually have anything to do with making money," she chuckled. This was a sobering and much needed view of her business.

Over the next three weeks, Jamie analyzed where each process could be pared, automated, delegated, or removed. She was like a ruthless plastic surgeon with an extra sharp scalpel. If there was fat to be cut, she was cutting it.

Step 4: Improve Your Processes

It was time to implement improvements. Jamie hired two new employees, handed them newly suggested processes, and gave them the authority to select the technology (within reason) that would work best to meet the requirements and the goal of the process.

She recognized that the investment of people/technology would keep her off the feast and famine rollercoaster and help her business financials trend upward.

Step 5: Control Your Processes

It's one thing to put in the process and another thing to control it. When I expect my Keurig to deliver my latte by 7:30am and all I get is hot water, I realize that it's because I forgot to put a coffee pod in the machine. When coffee pours onto my countertop rather than my cup, I know it's because I forgot to place a cup in the proper place.

This is the reason for control. Sometimes things go wrong. You might need a checklist to remember to do tasks like put water in the coffee pot. Usually when incidents happen, it's human error. Putting controls in place, without becoming a psychotic control freak, helps keep processes from failing.

After a year Jamie made minor changes to the processes. Today her business is thriving and she still uses the Room of Lost Trees to manage her business processes.

7

STRATEGY 4:
FORTIFY YOUR FUTURE

When my high school track and field coach told me that I would excel, I dreamed of wearing a gold medal on the Olympic stand. I was sure I'd break every record, from my first run in high school to my last as a professional athlete. I was on a mission to do whatever it took to be the best of the best. My first goal was to annihilate the school record for the mile.

On a Wednesday afternoon I joined the rest of the runners on the field. At the sound of my coach's whistle, I sprinted from the starting blocks and ran my heart out - for exactly one half mile. Turns out – I *hated* running.

My vision, mission, and goals weren't in-line with my expertise. I didn't see what my coach saw. I didn't like running, I wasn't a great runner, and I had no intention of getting better.

The difference between then and now was that today I had clarity on my expertise. The profit drought was mostly over and operations were in place, but I still needed a strategy to solidify my future.

Future Strategy

Your Future Strategy is just that. It defines the future of your business, how you make decisions, and the goals you plan to reach. But let me caution you before you start writing goals and visions - Superhero Syndrome is real! Far too many times I hear of entrepreneurs who set goals so lofty that Superman would get a bloody nose trying to reach them. There is nothing wrong with stretching, but you don't want to tear a hamstring along the way.

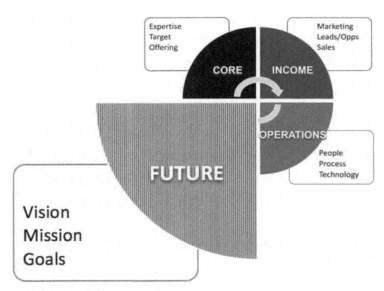

Figure 15 Future Strategy

Vision, Mission, and Goals Simplified

Years ago, while coming up with a Future Strategy, a marketing guru taught me the value of the Three Whys (3Y). This is the example he used:

Guru: What do you want to be when you grow up?
Child: The world's best firefighter
Guru: Why?
Child: So I can help people when bad things happen.
Guru: That's great. Why?
Child: So I can keep people safe – and keep them from losing their stuff.
Guru: Wow! That's cool, but why?
Child: So people learn how to keep fires from happening.

With the 3Ys the Guru had the vision, mission, and goals.

Vision: To be the world's best firefighter *To be a motivational speaker*
Mission: To stop bad things from happening *To help people*
Goals: Keep people safe; reduce loss; promote education. *To create a non-profit to help youth.*

It's so easy that even a little kid can do it. So why do many of the really big companies get it wrong? That isn't a rhetorical question. I really want to know. But in the meantime, we should get ours right.

Vision Statement

Walk into the grand lobby of any big Fortune 500 company and you will see a large mahogany wall plaque with the words *Our Vision* chiseled into the wood. Below the title, the lead-crystal tempered glass protects the aged paper inscribed with gold-leaf old English text. You instantly recognize the weight of the words you are about to read:

By creating value for our customers, we create value for our shareholders. It is our business to enthusiastically leverage other's world-class resources so that we may efficiently negotiate prospective paradigms to stay competitive in tomorrow's world. We recalibrate brands to broaden awareness, reframe global positions and reconnect with core customers. We turn innovation into impact.

Um...what? Is this a global positioning systems company providing customer service for astronauts? If so, that vision statement might mean something; but to the rest of us it's just gibberish. This type of convoluted vision statement is not an example to follow. The only use for statements like this is during a game of Meeting Bingo.

A good vision statement is simple and succinct. It drives future decisions and keeps everyone on board with what your organization's future looks like. Honest Tea's vision statement is *to be the source that creates and promotes great-tasting, healthier, organic beverages.*

Now imagine for a moment that you are the CEO of Honest Tea. You're considering a new farm to source Jasmine leaves for your Jasmine and Hibiscus tea. You discover that traces of propachlor could end up in the tea due to heavy pesticides used at the new farm. The supplier's prices are lower than all other bids. On one hand, using their leaves could increase your profit margin. On the other hand, using their leaves could cause you to lose your customer base.

Making this decision is easier than you think. As the CEO, all you have to do is use your vision statement to frame your decision: *Does propachlor promote great-tasting, healthier, organic beverages?*

If the answer is no (which it is) then you know exactly what to do.

Great vision statements aren't only for big companies either. The US District Court's Southern District of Florida's IT department has a vision statement that does exactly what it's supposed to do - guide decisions. Their statement is as follows:

To be the Information Technology Department in the US District Courts that consistently sets and exceeds technology benchmarks while remaining fiscally responsible, service oriented, and innovatively sound.

When James, the Director of IT, is asked about implementing something new, removing something old, or borrowing something blue he always asks four questions:

- Is this fiscally responsible?
- Will our customer be better served?
- Is this solution innovatively sound?
- Does this opportunity move us forward?

The answers drive his response. Every decision he makes must be in-line with the vision for his organization. As a result, his department is considered one of the most fiscally responsible, innovatively sound, and customer oriented IT Departments in the US District Courts.

Finally, your vision statement can promote innovation. Amazon's CEO, Jeff Bezos, uses their vision statement as a driving force for new ideas:

Our vision is to be earth's most customer centric company; to build a place where people can come to find and discover anything they might want to buy online.

The customer-centricity that Amazon touts in their vision statement drives innovation in the organization. Bezos wants to reduce the time that it takes to get small packages to customers from days to hours. His goal is to use drones to deliver packages under fifteen pounds, which he says makes up about 80% of the items purchase through Amazon.com.

Notice that all great vision statements include the words "to be" – almost as if someone is asking, "What do you want to be when you grow up?"

Your answer is your vision statement!

Mission Statement

If your vision statement creates your future, the mission statement reveals your action and, optionally, the purpose for that action. Google's Mission Statement is probably the best and most succinct I've seen in a long time:

Google's mission is to organize the world's information and make it universally accessible and useful.

If you've ever wondered why you're doing what you're doing, your mission statement should answer that question.

SMART Goals

Goals prepare you and your team for the term ahead. They help drive your day-to-day activities and promote focus in your organizations. Having goals is good, but not good enough.

SMART goals are specific, measurable, achievable, relevant, and time based.

Figure 16 SMART Goals

Let's say that you develop a goal for you team as follows: Each salesperson is to close $100K in sales.

That might sound pretty specific, but it leaves room for questions. What's the timeframe? Is this goal really achievable? Is the new product relevant to salespeople's target market or just a subset?

Look at the difference when we change this particular goal into a smart goal:

The goal for each new-widget salesperson is to increase their closing revenue by 20% over last year's numbers within the next 12 months. This can be achieved by introducing the new widgetized product line to customers in the highly-interested target market.

Notice how the SMART goal delivers more information and drives focus.

I was four strategies in, the B3 was done, and I was feeling good about my business foundation. The questions

74

regarding what I did, for whom I did it, and why my offering was valuable were easily answered.

When my phone did periodically ring, I could close the deal roughly 90% of the time. All I had to do was wait for the phone to ring.

So, I waited.

And waited.

And got super impatient.

Before long, old coffee slurping habits were new again. My sales drought clock had reset. I was having a *Field of Dreams* moment. I thought if I built a solid business foundation then sales would come.

They trickled in like a leaky faucet. While my business wasn't in famine mode, it was only surviving. I wanted it to thrive and explode with sales success. Hoping and waiting for the phone to ring didn't seem like a feasible business strategy.

Now that my foundation was in place, it was time to grow my business.

PART III
DAILY BUSINESS GROWTH

8

STRATEGY 5:
THE DAILY 6IX

I was always terrible at growing stuff. It didn't matter whether it was a cactus, a flower, or a goldfish. In my care, within a couple of weeks, the plant would wilt, the flower would die, and the goldfish would float. When a colleague gave me a ponytail palm, I was determined to make the relationship with the palm work. I started off strong by purchasing a new larger pot to replace the temporary one and fresh soil to keep the plant healthy. After following detailed instructions for transplant from one pot to another, I felt accomplished. This plant and I would be together for many years. I kept my side of the bargain – new pot, strong soil, great fertilizer, good light, and some water - now all it had to do was grow.

After three days I noticed that the plant looked a bit wilted. I couldn't believe it was giving up after all I'd done.

Like many daughters with life-and-death emergencies, I called my mom. She said, "Did you water it?"

I definitely poured water in there the first day. I also gave it premium soil and I threw my almost melted ice cubes in there whenever I passed by with a cup. How much water does it need? Seriously, I thought. My silence answered her question.

"A good pot and soil makes for a healthy foundation. But if you expect your plant to grow you must consistently care for it with water, fertilizer, and light. Consistently! All three!" she demanded.

After some trial and error, my ponytail palm pushed past the starvation hurdle and grew to be thriving greenery.

Just like the pot and soil weren't enough to make the plant grow, the foundation of my business needed consistent daily action if I wanted it to thrive.

The Ivy Lee Method

The Daily 6ix is actually a more strategic version of Ivy Lee's *Six Executive Actions*. The story is as follows:

By 1918, Charles M. Schwab was one of the richest men in the world. Schwab was the president of the Bethlehem Steel Corporation, the largest shipbuilder and the second-largest steel producer in America at that time. In 1918

Schwab was on a quest to increase the efficiency of his executive team. Schwab met with Ivy Lee, a highly-respected productivity expert.

Lee asked for 15 minutes with the executives. "How much will it cost me," Schwab asked. "Nothing," Lee said. "Unless it works. After three months, you can send me a check for whatever you feel it's worth to you."

The Ivy Lee Method was simple. At the end of each work day, write down the six most important things you need to accomplish tomorrow. Do not write down more than six tasks. Prioritize those six items in order of their true importance. When you arrive tomorrow, concentrate only on the first task. Work until the first task is finished before moving on to the second task. Approach the rest of your list in the same fashion. At the end of the day, move any unfinished items to a new list of six tasks for the following day. Repeat this process every working day.

The strategy sounded too simple, but Schwab and his executive team at Bethlehem Steel gave it a try. After three months, Schwab was so delighted with the progress his company had made that he called Lee into his office and wrote him a check for $25,000. A $25,000 check written in 1918 is the equivalent of a $400,000 check in 2016.

The Ivy Lee Method of prioritizing a to-do list seems simple and yet extremely effective.

I remember the first time Allen and I implemented Ivy Lee's method. We were like most other entrepreneurs - glad to work twenty hours a day for ourselves to avoid working eight hours for someone else. This mindset led us to spend entirely too much time on a single task and never reaching list completion. We also had a hard time figuring out what should be on the list and what shouldn't. My to-do list included tasks like: update website, design new business cards, or look at requests for proposal. At the time, those all seemed like mission-critical activities.

If Ivy Lee was judged based on our antics, he would have had to pay Schwab for time wasted. To stave off any entrepreneurial distractions and translation of exactly what Lee meant by "most important and prioritized tasks" we added a few guidelines to keep us on track.

The Daily 6ix Unplugged

Organizations that have strong growth numbers prioritize their focus in three areas:
- Producing income by moving the needle forward on current sales initiatives
- Building relationships that influence future business
- Innovation initiatives to drive new customers and keep current customers excited about offerings

Let's take a closer look at each area of focus.

Income Production

Unless an opportunity becomes a transaction, you are marketing - not selling. Unless your offering makes money, it is a hobby - not a business. Allen and I were doing everything except producing income.

Income Production had to be a priority in order to grow our business. At first this meant that Allen and I initiated all the sales calls, negotiated contracts, and closed business deals. As our company grew and we had a sales team, our personal income production tasks changed from direct sales to something more strategic. We opened new markets, helped a salesperson on a tough deal, and did whatever was necessary to move an opportunity through the sales cycle.

Regardless of our role or the size of our business, we found ways to make income production two of the six tasks that we completed every day.

Relationship Building

Remember your sleazy cousin Jimmy - the one who calls anytime he's joined the latest pyramid scheme? Well, he wants you to be the first on his new networking marketing team and he just left his eighth voicemail message. He can't wait to hear from you.

Oh YAY!

I can barely hear your excitement over all the eye-rolling.

By the way, that sinking feeling you get in your stomach whenever his number shows up on Caller ID is the same feeling your past clients get when you call them out of the blue.

They know you're not calling to build a relationship but instead to get something, to sell something, and they can hear the desperation in your voice from a mile away.

Richard Branson, Virgin CEO, once said, "Building meaningful business relationships is very important as people are a company's biggest asset." He wasn't just talking about internal assets; he was talking about past clients, current customers, and future opportunities.

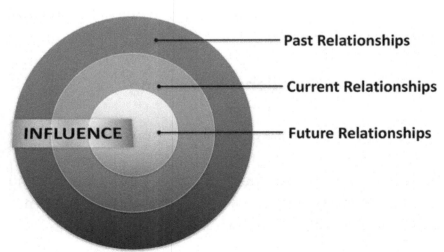

Figure 17 Relationship Influence Diagram

Relationship Building is more than networking or having coffee or calling someone out of the blue. You can begin relationships by connecting your connections, sharing new information with your network, and putting your connections in the direct path of opportunity.

Relationship building comes in several stages. They include anyone who you've already worked with and those with whom you want to work. Your job is to figure out how you will build *influential* relationships. Simple activities such as being a resource of information, connecting two people that can help each other, recognizing milestones of an individual, and dropping a periodic note in the mail all take less than five minutes and have huge impacts.

Smart entrepreneurs become so well-connected that their words carry the kind of weight that causes action. Their products and services stay at the top of someone's mind when opportunities arise. They become the go-to person for problem solving. I soon discovered that to be proficient in relationship building, all I had to do was be a fantastic listener, understand the quality of what others do, and the value they bring to my network. At the right time, I could leverage those connections for collaborative success within my network.

Professional Development

Innovation is a buzzword that many people associate with technology advancements. You had to use words like *polymorphism*, *encapsulation*, and *abstraction* in a joke that only a few people laughed at to truly be innovative. Then, low-tech companies like Airbnb, Uber, and Starbucks came along and people started calling them innovative. So, what gives?

Innovation has little to do with creating technology and more to do with improving the customer experience. If you use technology to make that happen, then great! If not, that's okay too.

Think about the experience of buying something at any store. You walk in, you select your purchase, you stand in line and wait...and wait...and wait. Finally, you give them your money.

Apple thought it was ridiculous to make people wait to give them money. So they changed the game. They leveraged technology to ensure that you could grab one of hundreds of Apple reps standing around and check out efficiently. No counters or cash registers. No waiting.

Professional Development is all about innovation. Think about your company's expertise and its offering. What do you know today that will be obsolete tomorrow? How will industry changes impact your future? What can you do to improve the customer experience?

All of these questions, and many more, are one part of professional development. It's how you think differently and share those unique thoughts with others.

Allen and I used to share weekly blogs. We'd learn something new about business intelligence and pass those lessons on to our customers. Our customers would then give us new information and alternate points of view to share with our network. This constant reciprocal learning and sharing of information allowed us to stay on the cutting edge in our industry.

To keep professional development at top of mind, at the beginning of every week we'd post a note that read: *How can we make the customer experience better in*...and then we'd fill in the blank. For example: we might enter *create better dashboards so that our customer can have a clearer view into the activities of their business.* Then for the rest of the week our two professional development tasks included spit-balling analytical dashboards until we came up with an article titled, "The Future of Analytical Dashboards." Reader responses to our article gave us ammunition for new innovations, which spawned more profits in our business, as well as, next week's professional development tasks.

The Daily 6ix Guidelines

I don't generally follow rules, but in my own handwriting I saw the word *RULES*. Maybe I knew in my future desperation that rules would be necessary to my success. Underneath the giant red letters, I had written the word *Guidelines* in thick blue Sharpie. I wrote everything for a reason.

I was speaking to my future self! I could follow a guideline, but always felt that rules were meant to be broken… hard!

The rules were straight forward: Create and prepare to execute your plan, follow your plan even when you don't want to, and limit the amount of time when you can execute each portion of your plan.

Rule #1: Plan Accordingly

Like every other New Year's resolution junkie, I purchased a $100 per month, 12 months, non-cancellable, chalk-flavored shake drinking, $500 sneaker-buying — gym membership.

And like all rookie members reenacting the excitement of the first day of school, I set the alarm to wake up earlier than usual, put on my shiny new outfit, and wandered from one workout station to the next. I admired the gym equipment and commenced fantastic conversations at the smoothie bar about the 10lbs of holiday weight that I was going to work off. I ogled people in the spin class while they worked up a sweat to head-banging hip-hop at the command of a Marine Corps wannabe drill instructor.

But I never actually lifted a weight, joined a spin class,

or reaped the benefits of my $1200 investment.

The same is true of The Daily 6ix. You'll waste money, time, and reap zero benefits unless you make The Daily 6ix a priority. It only takes two steps to be ruthless: 1) Create a plan. 2) Relentlessly follow that plan.

Now before you get to work on that list, remember this: just because you have a plan doesn't mean that you're immediately skilled at executing every part of the plan to perfection.

At the gym I could plan on doing 35 reverse-pull Roman dead-lift squats with 200 pound weights. I could plan to develop the type of buns that could turn charcoal into diamonds with a single tushy squeeze. However, if my form is off the only development will be a grapefruit sized hernia and a viral YouTube video earning comments like, "Wow, I didn't think it was physically possible to simultaneously bite your own ass and tuck your knee behind your ear. But look, at 1:35 - she totally nails it!"

Even a thoroughbred racehorse learns how to trot. You will get better over time, but you have to be consistent in your actions to do so. Here is the good news:

- No one has ever received an injury greater than a wicked paper cut while executing the Daily 6ix.
- No matter your skill level, with consistent execution (and Band-Aid-covered fingertips) you will get better and reach your goals.

The ultimate goal is to plan for and execute The Daily 6ix every day. But some days The Daily 6ix will be The 4our or The Thr33. For example, when I'm flying from the US to London on a nine-hour flight, it's tough to execute relationship building or income production in my normal way. I might choose to skip it and focus on the speech that I'm about to give in front of three thousand people.

The point is that you should plan at night for the next day. Then put all the elements in place to execute that plan. Some days you'll do a little less and that's okay. It's important to mold the Daily 6ix to meet your business.

Rule #2: Ruthlessly Follow Your Plan (even when it hurts)

Avoidance is easy, unless you have a stalker - then you need paperwork, pepper spray, and an open carry permit. By practicing The Daily 6ix you will discover where your savant-like strengths lie and weed out your remaining weaknesses.

Like most humans you will gravitate towards your strengths and avoid your weaknesses like a pissed off porcupine. That means instead of working through a challenge, at one point or another, you will find yourself falling back into comfortable old habits. But comfort is the enemy of growth. Dr. Abraham Twerski shared a story about a lobster that really drives this point home.

A lobster lives inside of a rigid shell. As the lobster grows the shell becomes very uncomfortable. The lobster hides under a rock from predators where he sheds the old shell and develops a new one. Eventually, that shell becomes uncomfortable and the process of shedding and developing a new shell starts again. The stimulus for the lobster to shed and grow is discomfort.

Here's a tip: When you find yourself cradled snugly in the comfort zone of *I don't like to do that kind of work so I will pretend it doesn't exist* - fight your way out! Be persistent! Be ruthless! Be a killer of cramped comfort! And above all, ruthlessly follow your plan.

Rule #3: Highly Focused Healthy Limits

When Allen and I first started using The Daily 6ix we were more bullheaded than ruthless. We would set goals too high and push ourselves to the point of burnout.

During one lengthy stint, Allen only worked on income producing calls with the goal of getting a sales meeting with a top executive willing to sign a ten-million-dollar deal. He wouldn't move on to relationship building until he reached his semi-impossible goal. After a long stint of cold-calling frustration and failure he declared, "All telephones shall be banned for use when making phone calls!"

To make matters worse, our current cold-calling marathon antics didn't coincide with our professional history. We didn't leverage lessons learned from past mistakes.

As programmers, Allen and I knew the value of walking away from a problem to clear your head. I would spend hours figuring out how to correct a random coding error. After threatening the monitor, assaulting the keyboard, and throwing the mouse, I would take a break. I'd grab a water, take a walk, or go to lunch. Upon returning to my console, the problem would invariably reveal itself in just a few seconds.

We also discovered that from a health perspective it was good to get up from our desks and move at least once per hour. We wanted to stay healthy, not use all of our ROI on broken keyboards and damaged mice – we needed to avoid burnout. Vilfredo came into play.

Vilfredo Pareto found that eighty percent of the land in Italy was owned by twenty percent of the population in 1906. And while that's pretty interesting, finding that the 80/20 distribution happens a lot is really interesting. Like the fact that eighty percent of your time on your cellphone is spent talking to twenty percent of your top ten contacts. Or like the fact that two of every ten of your customers represents eighty percent of your sales. And twenty percent of your time produces eighty percent of your results.

To leverage the Pareto Principle in The Daily 6ix, allot

twenty percent of your day to focus on a specific work area. That means you get twenty percent of your day to focus on Income Production. And that twenty percent will deliver eighty percent of your revenue. Yep! That's it.

Using a typical eight-hour workday, you would get ninety-six minutes per day (or twenty percent of an eight-hour day) to focus on making money. Another ninety-six minutes to build amazing relationships. And the final ninety-six minutes for professional development. What you do with the rest of your day is totally up to you.

Since Allen and I wanted to find ways to reduce eye strain, back aches, and hot ears from holding the phone for ninety-six minutes, we split the ninety-six-minute task into two forty-eight minutes' segment. We'd work on income production for forty-eight minutes, then walk away and clear our heads for twelve minutes. We'd complete the next forty-eight minutes of work and then take another twelve-minute break before starting on forty-eight minutes of relationship building.

Finally, we looked at scarcity. In 1975, researchers wanted to know how people would value cookies in two identical glass jars. One jar had ten cookies while the other contained only two. Though the cookies and jars were identical, participants valued more the cookies in the near-empty jar.

This is the scarcity principle at play. It essentially means that people tend to place higher value on an object that is scarce and a lower value on a more readily available and abundant object. No wonder marketing guru Robert Cialdini cites 'Scarcity' as one of the six golden persuasion principles in his book *Influence*. When combined with 'Urgency', which is essentially the other side of the same coin, the two make for a potent weapon for increasing e-commerce sales.

We see this principle at work almost all the time and Allen and I were both victims of it. Even though Allen and I had a fully paid, two-year membership to 24 Hour Fitness, it hadn't seen either of us since the first week we signed up. To make matters worse, I had a full gym in my home gathering dust and periodically, a load of laundry.

It wasn't until I joined an outdoor boot camp where my participation was limited to ninety minutes between the hours of 6:00 am and 7:30 pm, that the scarcity principle really made sense.

I hated running, push-ups, planks, and squats. I hated them even more in the high humidity and hot summers of Fort Lauderdale, Florida. And yet, every day I showed up fully prepared and ready to plank, push-up, run, and squat. I couldn't put it off until later because there was no later. If I dared to show up later, then I could lose my spot or endure a lower return on investment. After all, I paid for a ninety-minute workout and if I'm even one minute late, I would not get a full ninety-minute workout.

During the entire time that I participated in the boot camp, my home gym remained untouched and Allen never attended 24 Hour Fitness. I knew my home gym would be there twenty-four hours a day, seven days per week, waiting for me to give it some attention. I ignored it because I knew I could use it later.

Rule of Rewarding Work: Set Milestones and Goals

The first thing that I thought when reading The Daily 6ix rules was, Holy crap Batman! Six more hours' worth of work? I guess sleep is unnecessary.

Fear not! You can sleep and still employ The Daily 6ix.

The Daily 6ix shouldn't take six hours unless you're having an extremely bad day. Each work area, such as income production, must have a goal. When working your forty-eight minutes, ask yourself, "What do I want to achieve in the next forty-eight minutes?" The answer must be specific, measurable, relevant to your work, and achievable within forty-eight minutes. You can have a sales conversation that moves the needle twenty points, close deals, or make ten calls.

The best thing about goals is that they set a precedent over time. If you reach your goal within the forty-eight-minute mark, then you can take a break for twelve minutes and then get to your next forty-eight-minute task. For example, if your first two phone calls turn into sales and your goal was to close two sales for both forty-eight minute tasks, then you are done with income production work for the day. Congrats! You win! Game over!

On the other hand, once you reach the forty-eight-minute mark, even if you haven't reached the goal, you must stop. To continue would likely be a waste of valuable time - at least according to Pareto.

What The Daily 6ix Day Looks Like

The Daily 6ix is meant to be strategic and actionable. Take a look at a typical 6ixer's list.

7:30 - 7:35am Relationship Building 1
- Connect Assaf of RankAdvisor.com to Janet for website development and business app work.
- Goal - Send email and make recommendation.

7:40 - 7:45am Relationship Building 2
- Send Postcards - Topic - Congrats on PMP Exam to: Jenna Marshall of Merck, 10105 N Main Street, Newark, NJ, 10102
- Topic - Thought this would make you laugh too: Tom McHill - San Diego Water - 5250 Water Works Way - San Diego, CA 22445

Goal: Move Relationship forward by 2 points.
7:30 - 7:35am Relationship Building 1

8:00 - 8:30am - Income Production 1

- Help Marlene with Cochrane deal pricing to get to a close or walk decision @ 8:00am
- Coach John on Value Prop for FWA to move the deal to contract @ 8:10am
- Review EXA proposal. Add deal sweetener if close by EOD @ 8:20am

Goal: Assist one deal to close by EOD or get 20 points closer to close.

8:45 - 9:15am Income Production 2
- Have sales conf. call with Joanne in LV to move the needle by 10 points @ 8:45am
- Close or kill deal with Courtney @ 8:55am
- Help Cat with 3 open proposals. Get at least 2 to close by EOD. Other to move forward 10 points in pipeline @ 9:05am

Goal: Move at least one deal forward in the pipeline

9:30 - 9:45am Professional Development 1
- Reach out to target market re: new offering. Get an understanding of their challenges, ideas, and insights for weekly article.

9:45 - 10:00am Professional Development 2
- Put together article outline. Goal: Outline 1 main point. 3 supporting points.

Notice how the Daily 6ix was done in just over 2 hours.

There were breaks to check email, get coffee, etc. This 6ixer's day starts with relationship building. He's sending emails and postcards which don't rely on people being in the office. Income production happens right at the start of the day, and professional development is gathering information and new insights about an article he plans to write for his target market.

I was ready. My blueprint was solid and I knew exactly what my next workday would look like. It was time to make profits on purpose.

9

BUMPS IN THE ROAD

I finally felt that I had the tools to move in the right direction, quickly. In hindsight, it seemed silly to struggle so much. My trend line before I developed a strong business foundation resembled a flat line with a periodic blip on the screen. After I had a strong business foundation there were more blips on the screen, but nothing I would call a trend. I had taken life-saving measures, but now we needed to get the patient up and moving. It was time to put The Daily 6ix in action every day.

For the first time since starting my new business, I held a list of opportunities whose challenges I could confidently solve. That night I wrote out the Daily 6ix tasks, start times, durations, and specifics. I was excited about getting to work on Monday morning.

My first official day on The Daily 6ix started with income

production. I reached out to potential prospects or as Seth Godin calls them - suspects. My goal for each income production work area was to have a positive conversation in order to convert a suspect into a strong prospect. Within 15 minutes of calling, I had reached my first goal and took a 12-minute break to check emails. I started my next round of phone calls and within 20 minutes, another suspect became a prospect who was also interested in a proposal. After 35 minutes of phone calls, there were two interested prospects on my list. Based the law of averages, I could conservatively have 10 proposals out and 1 closed contract within a couple of weeks.

Relationship building was next on the docket. A list of contacts from Microsoft, Google, Exelon, Johnson Controls, and LN gave me pause. These aren't the types of companies that will help fill my funnel with the right types of opportunities. I quickly brushed off relationship building and moved into professional development.

I spent 22 minutes learning about a new CRM tool, AgileCRM, that helps entrepreneurs up their relationship building and income production game. I immediately began outlining an article on the new tool.

Two hours into my day and The Daily 6ix was complete; well, kinda complete. Relationship building had thrown a wrench into my plans but in my mind that was okay. I didn't like networking anyway.

My phone rang during the early hours of July 25th. I wiped the toothpaste from my mouth, "This is Dawnna."

"Oh my God! Dawnna? *The* Dawnna St Louis? It can't be! I thought you died!" The woman's serious tone turned into laughter. "It's Barbara Manson from LN. I haven't heard from you in ages."

Barbara was the Marketing Executive from LN that hired my company 18 months before. She was also the person that I'd blown off of my relationship building list two weeks ago - tasks I still hadn't completed. I was a little embarrassed that I hadn't reached out to her to keep up, but justified my actions by reminding myself that she was not my target market anymore and I hated networking.

"I've been seeing all of your articles about entrepreneurship on LinkedIn. We would love for you to come out and share The 6ix Strategies with our user group." At first I was a little confused about why a large global organization like LN would be the least bit interested in The 6ix Strategies or entrepreneurship. Then Barbara explained that LN has user-group conferences for their users who are business owners. Within 90 minutes of our conversation Barbara signed the agreement and submitted a payment.

I sat perplexed. I ignored relationship building and large companies like LN for the past few weeks. Was I off target on my market? By ignoring my past clients and relationship building, was I throwing the baby out with the bathwater?

Later that night I was sharing the LN story with my son Brytt. He told me a story that made the whole thing make sense.

"Mom, what would you print with a 3D printer?" he asked.

"I don't know. 3D stuff," I said.

He rolled his eyes. "No really think about it. Today you went to Lowes to get sprinkler heads. You also picked up a plastic drawer organizer from Organized Living. And you cracked your case for your iPhone. What if you could just print that kind of stuff?"

I laughed. "Yeah. I guess I would. I hate going to the store for knick-knacks." My mind reeled. "I could print letter openers, scissors, plastic forks... a CAR!"

Brytt continued. "Well, there is a guy that built a 3D printer. He wanted to help architects produce their models faster, reduce the cost of developing models, and make changes easier by recycling and reprinting. It uses some type of plastic. While it's cool for architects, other industries are interested in his printer as well. The medical industry uses it to make prosthetic limbs and maybe one day they'll use organic material to make organs. The military is looking at potentially making weapons and armor for troops. The automotive industry is looking at printing car parts on demand. The guy who developed the 3D printer was trying to solve a single problem for a single customer. The rest of the world is figuring out how to use it to solve theirs. The

6ix Strategies solve a single problem for you and your main customers - entrepreneurs. Maybe it is your job to share it so that other people can figure out how to use it to solve their problems too," he said before heading up to his room.

My mind exploded. It wasn't up to me to decide how people would use my expertise. It was up to me to share it and let people determine how they can apply it to their business. Suddenly I had a reason to reach back to former clients.

10

NECESSITY IS THE MOTHER OF
OMG! I NEED AN IDEA

The biggest problem I ran into when implementing The Daily 6ix was that I really liked to do professional development and hired someone to do the parts of income production that I didn't prefer. But I knew that only focusing on professional development wouldn't have a positive impact on the bottom line. This is the same as improving your vocal range from six to eight octaves in the shower. If no one hears you then did you really improve? And even more importantly, if the right people don't hear you then who's going to buy your song on iTunes?

I had to come up with smarter and more innovative ways to move relationship building into the mix and hiring someone to build relationships for me felt like marketing. I figured the smartest thing to do was leverage my greatest strength - professional development against my greatest weakness - relationship building.

I looked at all of the articles I'd written about entrepreneurship and matched them, based on interest, with people that I wanted to do business with and those who had already done business with me. I hated calling people or sending out newsletter emails to say, "Hey! Look at my article!" So I had to find a smarter way to reach them.

I tried printing the articles and mailing them to the select group over the first couple of weeks. I printed 100 articles. Addressed 100 envelopes. Stamped each envelope and put them in my car to go to the post office. After 3 weeks of riding in my backseat, I figured they weren't going to make it there by themselves and I chucked the idea.

Then I decided to utilize the method of email newsletter. Everyone else was telling me that I needed a list and that it was important to keep my list well-oiled with new content. After 2 weeks 30% of the people unsubscribed. Plus, a newsletter felt like marketing, not relationship building. Just when I relented to the fact that I was going to fail at relationship building, an idea landed on my desk that completely changed my mind.

My husband, James, walked in the house with the mail. As usual, he tossed everything that was junk and dropped two items on my desk. The first - a check from a client. The second - a postcard. I put the check aside and picked up the postcard. It was from the Mercedes Benz dealership around the corner from my home. My longtime friend and salesperson, Abel, was retiring and had invited me to his party.

And then it hit me. Postcards! If that invitation would have come in a Mercedes Benz envelope, it likely would have found the trash can along with the other junk mail. But this was instant, easy, and in my hands. Not only did I read it, but I RSVP'd and attended the function.

One postcard. Three sentences. Instant action. That was how I would build relationships.

The next week, my relationship building tasks consisted of sending one postcard per task or two per business day. Each postcard was limited to three sentences. With addressing, stamping, writing, and sending both tasks took me a total of ten minutes.

While most postcards were basic, some were fun. One postcard was made out of pinewood and had instructions to pop out the pieces and make a little airplane. My client was a huge lover of anything flying, so when he got it he immediately called me. Another postcard was a 3D pop-up of the word *CONGRATS* for someone who had just passed the PMP exam (which I discovered on LinkedIn).

Sending the postcards made me feel good about completing my relationship building tasks every week. Getting positive responses, along with referrals for new business, let me know that it was definitely working.

PART IV
CONTINUOUS IMPROVEMENT

11

STRATEGY 6:
KAIZEN

Dan Justice owns Justice Printing, a commercial printing company in Washington, DC. For the first two years in business Justice Printing targeted government events. Unfortunately, his business was struggling, so he decided to give The Daily 6ix a try. During his first ten weeks as a 6ixer he reached out to four hundred leads. One hundred leads were professional athletic organizations. One hundred leads were advertising agencies. One hundred were event planning companies specializing in government events - his prime target market. And one hundred were large companies in his local market. His process was well-defined.

Dan created a spreadsheet with a category called Industry and four data points: professional athletic organizations, advertising agencies, event planning companies for government, and Fortune 500 companies.

Using this information, Dan took a few measurements per data point such as:

- How many suspects became prospects?
- How many prospects moved past the 50% mark in your sales process?
- How many prospects became sales?
- How many prospects are still interested?
- How long did it take for a prospect to become a sale?
- How many touch points were required to transform a suspect into a sale?

Dan entered his numbers in the spreadsheet. His expectations were that event planning companies for government agencies would have garnered the highest sales. But it turned out that advertising agencies and Fortune 500 companies in his local area outperformed that data point. Upon further inspection, Dan discovered that the government market was oversaturated and lower priced than his offering.

With this information Dan could make better strategic decisions. He could go back to his Core Strategy, look at his target market and determine a better marketing strategy to yield higher results. In less than three months Dan had insight into what he should start doing, stop doing, and keep doing.

Figuring out when to stop, when to start, or when to

keep going can be difficult. It's like heading to a four-way intersection with no traffic signals or signs. Move when you shouldn't and you're hit. Take too long, you miss a chance to go, and the guy behind you lays on his horn. Keep up the pace without looking both ways and you have to hope that nothing goes wrong.

Hope is not a strategy.

Before I figured out what I needed to start, stop, and keep doing, I needed clarity into my current performance.

Set Your Baseline

When you initially implement The Daily 6ix, the ten-week mark is the perfect point at which to take measurements. Over ten weeks, if you followed The Daily 6ix to the letter, you will have completed one hundred income production tasks, one hundred relationship building tasks, and one hundred professional development tasks. You have worked long enough to analyze your efforts and can take a couple of weeks to make improvements before the next quarter starts.

To measure your progress, first we must collect your data from each category. In Dan's case, he looked at all of his income production work and selected industry as the first category. Then he further narrowed down that category into four data points.

From here, Dan used his own metrics to measure how each data point was performing. This first measurement is called your baseline. Any time you take a measurement on the same data point you are identifying a trend over time.

There are other factors that Dan could take into consideration, for example, the US Government is less busy at the very beginning of a fiscal year. During summer breaks and lulls in political fundraising there are less events to market. Dan may consider reviewing his government efforts when things are busier. When he does, Dan would compare his current performance to his baseline to discover if there is enough of a difference to continue marketing to that target.

Measuring your progress should happen once per quarter. Ten weeks of activity and two weeks of planned corrections will allow you to have a clearer view into activities that work, those that don't work, and new activities that you want to try.

Continuous Improvement

Ever since I got the call from LN ten weeks ago, I'd been staying true to The Daily 6ix. This was the perfect time to measure my success with one hundred of each activity under my belt.

Over the ten weeks, if I reached out to three hundred suspects, one hundred would become prospects. Of those one-hundred prospects twenty-two would have a strong chance of closing. And eight will close immediately. I was closing ten percent of all suspects and one third of all prospects.

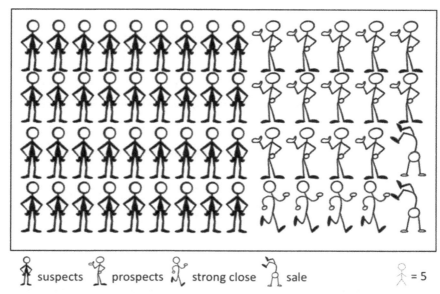

suspects   prospects   strong close   sale   = 5

Figure 18 Ten Week Sales Diagram

"Not bad," I thought.

For the first time I had numbers to work with. If I wanted to keep the same pace, I just had to keep what I was already doing. However, if I wanted to add fifty percent to my bottom line, then I needed to either add fifty percent more suspects or get better leads.

Relationship building was the Achilles Heel of my business. To network felt like I was surrounded by assassins using business cards as ninja throwing stars and their hand-shakes as takedown maneuvers. The conversations felt inauthentic and forced. I always had to get past the bluster and bullshit to find the real person whose business problem needed a real solution.

To my surprise though, relationship building was very strong for me. Admittedly, all of the postcards I sent out were to past business associates. But there were a few other opportunities that made significant headway. A local news anchor, Jim Berry, and I accidentally met at a family style rib spot. We talked, laughed, and exchanged business cards. After a few months of chatting and exchanging emails, his reference to an opportunity turned into new business. Relationship building added 28% to my bottom line.

Finally, my professional development numbers were in. Over the past ten weeks I had delivered new information about my products and services in the form of articles on various social media outlets. From my professional development activities, nine new prospects found their way into my pipeline, and two of those prospects led to new business.

In just ten weeks, three days, two hours, and nine minutes I had closed eighteen deals. I was offering my expertise to my target audience and using my Professional Development activities to ensure that specific target audience was aware of my expertise and offerings through educational articles.

Over the next several months, I knew exactly what to expect. One of every three calls would lead to an interest in my offerings. My phone would ring a couple of times a week in response to a personalized postcard. And my pipeline would fill because of an article or two posted in just the right places at just the right time.

My business had exited famine and was trending upwards. Everything was fantastic.

12

BONUS:
ACCOUNTABILITY & MASTERMIND

Are you really doing The Daily 6ix or are you just telling me that you're doing it? This is the question I asked my colleague, Sandra, who was also an entrepreneur in her own right. She and I seemed to experience peaks and valleys in our business at the same time and we started The Daily 6ix in tandem. As Sandra peered up from her iPad, my raised brow and squinty eyes let her know that an answer asserting a perfect execution of The Daily 6ix would never convince me.

Acting more as a mind-reader than CEO Sandra retorted, "We should have a weekly meeting for The Daily 6ix so that we can hold each other accountable. In fact, I know two other business owners that could use an accountability and mastermind group." My eyebrows lowered. My eyes widened.

Sensing my openness to the idea, she continued. "Think about it. We'd be able to share ideas, get expert advice from non-competing colleagues, develop partnerships, and spend less time reinventing the wheel. Imagine what it would do for your relationship building - I know how much you love that."

Sandra's idea was brilliant. We named it *The 6ix Accountability and Mastermind Group* (6A&M). All we needed to do was create a mastermind formula that worked. After several bumps in the road, we finally landed on guidelines that delivered results.

6A&M Member Guidelines

Our vision was to be a safe place and source of accountability, guidance, and ideas for business owners who followed The Daily 6ix. To do this our mission was to create an exclusive forum where business owners could share successes, failures, goals, opportunities, and get help to reach the next level of their personal best. The goal was to interview and invite up four additional members to become 6ixers.

To become a participating 6ixer, the prospect would need to complete the B3 and adhere to The Daily 6ix for ten weeks before being interviewed by the group. Also, a 6ixer would need to be noncompetitive with other 6ixers. In other words, a printing company could not join the same 6ixer group as another printing company doing the same type of printing. Industry exclusivity was critical to minimizing competition and maximizing referrals.

A prospect had to be a cultural fit. A chauvinist who thought I should be in the kitchen making him a sammich would likely cause a rift in the group and not be a fit. Information hoarders who saw other members in the group as competitors or as future customers, rather than partners, would also not be a fit. Finally, we wanted prospects that were focused on and willing to work towards their goals - not just create a vision board and pop bonbons while watching TV all day.

Within a few months the 6A&M was underway. Dre Baldwin, of DreAllDay.com, was a former international basketball player who taught mental toughness to top professional athletes and business leaders. His speech entitled *The Third Day* changed my life!

John Peragine, of OsirisPapers.com, was a writing coach and ghostwriter who knew how to pull top-selling tomes of knowledge out of his client's head and get them onto Amazon's best-seller list. He had an unmatched ability to find someone's authentic voice and story.

Jared Sirus of Sirus Machines developed software for self-driving vehicles. Now, if only he could get me to balance on a hover board.

For the first time in my new career my business felt complete. I had a daily strategy that could be measured, analyzed, and improved. I had a weekly accountability and mastermind group that supported my success, helped me through roadblocks, and sparked my imagination with new ideas. I knew that people were the core of good business and now I had the right people who were as committed to me as I was to them.

There was only one thing left to do - give myself a reminder. So, Friday afternoon on September 2012, I taped a note to the edge of my monitor that read:

"To predict the future of business, you must create it".
Stay true to The 6ix."

APPENDIX – FORMS AND SAMPLES

CORE STRATEGY

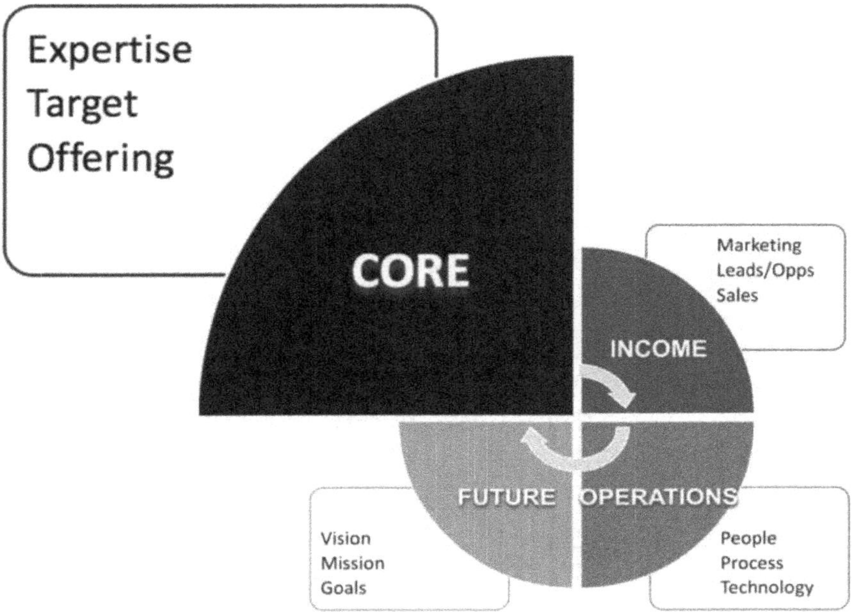

Expertise
Target
Offering

CORE

Marketing
Leads/Opps
Sales

INCOME

FUTURE OPERATIONS

Vision
Mission
Goals

People
Process
Technology

Figure 19 Core Strategy

The Core defines the organization's expertise, the target market that wants that expertise, and the offerings used to deliver that expertise to the target market.

The next few pages will allow you to clearly and concisely define your Core Strategy. When defining your Core Strategy consider only one area of expertise, target market, and offering. Adding too many will exponentially increase your work. For example: If you had three areas of expertise and two target markets then you complete six B3 blueprints.

Define Your Expertise:

What do you know that others would benefit from knowing?

Process Design + ~~Business~~ Planning

What do you do that others would benefit from doing?

Process Design

What do you have that others would benefit from having?

Experience

In one sentence, define your expertise.

Process Design can map out your

Life

Define Your Target Market:

Who wants to and will benefit from your expertise? Consider the industry, role, financial situation, etc. of your target market.

Sales Industry, Management

What issue does your target market have that your expertise could solve? What do they want to know, do, or have?

Customer, Employer Retention

Organization

Profitability

Long term vision

What are your target market's frustrations, fears and failures, desires, and breakthroughs? Complete the FAD table.

Frustrations	Desires
Fears/Failures	**Breakthroughs**

Define Your Offering

How will you deliver your expertise to your target market? What will you offer at higher levels and what price can your target market bear? How does offering provide a solution to your target market?

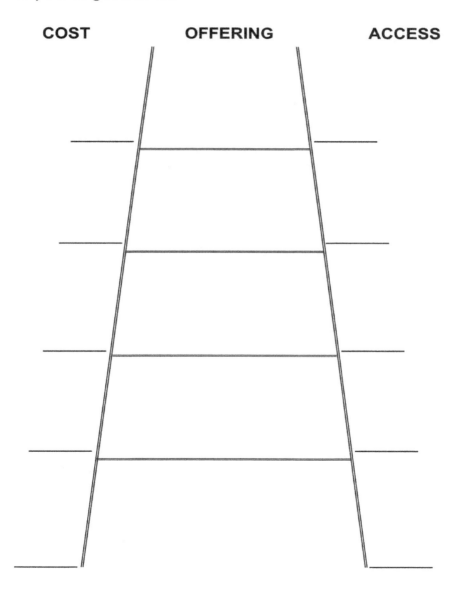

COST   OFFERING   ACCESS

Sample Diagram: Core Strategy

Frustrations

No natural relief from CP. Too many drugs prescribed. They are pitied. Can't enjoy life without drugs.

Desires

Relief without drugs. Normal family life and activities. Lower stress. Money to enjoy life.

Fears/Failures

Opioid addiction. Miss out on life. No money for prescription. Shunned by others.

Breakthroughs

Membership plan for chronic pain sufferers to get therapeutic massage that relieves CP.

PREMIUM   **PRIVATE**

Everything below + 4x/wk., platinum members lounge, dedicated masseuse, free access classes and private events, wine and dine free lunch.

Everything below + 2x/wk. access, premiere (room, bed, oil, time) svc, priority and free access to all classes, partner perks, discount lunch.

Everything below + 4x/mo. access, upgraded spa services (room, bed, oil, time), discounted invitation to classes.

Monthly membership to entry level program. General access 2x per mo. First access to deals for members only.

Blog, Articles, 15 minute consultation, free trials, video presentations.

COST   ACCESS

FREE   **PUBLIC**

132

EXPERTISE

Do: Massages
Have: Massage techniques that temporarily relieve chronic pain
Know: How to temporarily relieve chronic pain through massage

TARGET MARKET

Who benefits: CP suffers of back pain, Arthritis, Headache, Multiple sclerosis, Shingles, etc
Problems solved: stress, lack of human touch, too many drugs.
What are the FADs: see FAD diagram

OFFERING

How will you deliver your expertise? What is your cost, offering, and access?

See CAS diagram

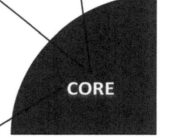

CORE

INCOME STRATEGY

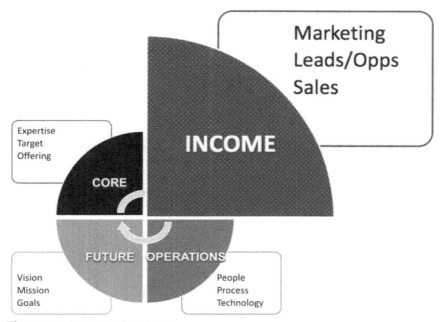

Figure 20 Income Strategy

The Income Strategy determines how an organization sets itself out at an expert, how it communicates offerings to its target market (marketing), how those communications translate into opportunities, and how those opportunities become sales.

Remember that we said that repetition is good. You really should not be reinventing the wheel in this section. Some of the answers here, should be the same answers defined in your Core Strategy. For example: The reason your target market wants your solution should be the same in your Core Strategy and Marketing Strategy. In your Marketing Strategy, however, we will dig deeper and understand why they are interested logically and emotionally.

Define Your Marketing Strategy

Why does your target market want your expertise?
Quantify this in terms of more or less Time, Money, Work.

_____

_____

_____

_____

_____

_____

_____

_____

_____

Why does your target market want your expertise? Qualify this emotionally. How will they be better?

Complete the 4P (Product, Placement, Price, Promotion) table below for each of your offerings:

Offering #1:

Price:

Emotional Triggers:

Logical Triggers

What will your target market learn with this offering?

Where will you place it:

Offering #2:

Price:

Emotional Triggers:

Logical Triggers

What will your target market learn with this offering?

Where will you place it:

Offering #3:

Price:

Emotional Triggers:

Logical Triggers

What will your target market learn with this offering?

Where will you place it:

Offering #4:

Price:

Emotional Triggers:

Logical Triggers

What will your target market learn with this offering?

Where will you place it:

Offering #5:

Price:

Emotional Triggers:

Logical Triggers

What will your target market learn with this offering?

Where will you place it:

Define Your Leads Strategy

Define the attributes of a strong lead

_____

_____

_____
Define your lead to opportunity funnel.

_____

_____

_____

_____

_____

_____

_____

Which touchpoint in the Opportunity Funnel has the highest high dollar and low dollar conversion rate?

_____

_____

What percentage of leads become opportunities?

_____

_____

_____

How can you increase the quality of your leads and the conversion ratio?

_____

_____

_____

_____

Define Your Sales Strategy

Define your opportunity to sales funnel.

_____

_____

_____

_____

_____

_____

Which touchpoint in the Sales Funnel has the highest high dollar and low dollar conversion rate?

_____

_____

_____

_____

How can you increase the quality of your opportunities and the conversion ratio?

What is the jump off point that moves a sale from one level to a higher level?

Sample Diagram: Income Strategy

MARKETING

Why does your TM want your expertise quantifiably: Reduced stress and pain by 25%. Why does your TM want your expertise emotionally: Feel better, be pampered, get more than you expected, feel beautiful, feel special, have what others desire, be better.
Define your 4P: See 4P Document

LEADS

Strong Lead Attributes: CP, extra income, flex schedule, holistic
Opportunity Funnel: Free -> Class-> Consultation-> Trial
Highest Conversion: $ Trial / $$$$ Consultation
Improvement: Don't offer Trial and coupons.

SALES

Strong Op Attributes: Strong lead that attended consultation.
Sales Funnel: Sign up with trial; trail to membership; increase member level
Highest Conversion: $$$$ Mid-level membership and $ Trial Membership
Improvement: Remove trial bonus from low membership level.

INCOME

OPERATIONS STRATEGY

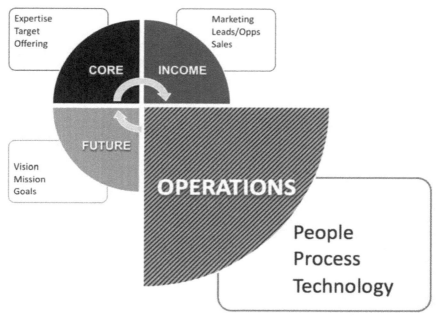

Figure 21 Operations Strategy

The Operations section identifies the people, processes, and technologies required to deliver the best experience to the customer while streamlining operations within the business. These questions help define operations at a high level.

Defining your processes is the best way to determine where you can streamline with people or technology.

Define Your Operations Optimization Strategy

Step 1: List all of the processes that you complete in your organization.

Repeat Steps 2 – 6 for each process identified in Step 1
Step 2: Define each step of a single process, the predecessors, the successors, and who (role not name) is responsible for the step.

Step 3: Measure the duration of each step.

Step 4: Analyze process. Where can you leverage technology to increase efficiency? How can the process be shifted for better results? Where do you see the most waste?

Step 5: Improve process. Define each step of your improved process, the predecessors, the successors, and who (role not name) is responsible for the step, and times. Take a note of time savings.

Step 5a: Based on your improvements, list the new technology or people or process you need. When do you need them?

Step 6: Control the process. What type of human intervention must occur for this process to remain constant?

Sample Diagram: Operations Strategy

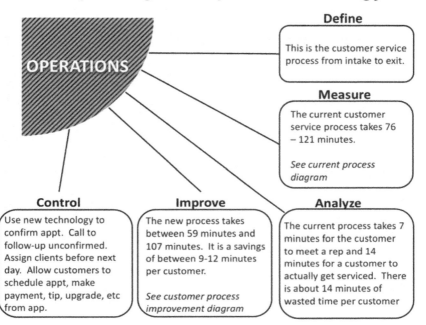

Define

This is the customer service process from intake to exit.

Measure

The current customer service process takes 76 – 121 minutes.

See current process diagram

OPERATIONS

Control

Use new technology to confirm appt. Call to follow-up unconfirmed. Assign clients before next day. Allow customers to schedule appt, make payment, tip, upgrade, etc from app.

Improve

The new process takes between 59 minutes and 107 minutes. It is a savings of between 9-12 minutes per customer.

See customer process improvement diagram

Analyze

The current process takes 7 minutes for the customer to meet a rep and 14 minutes for a customer to actually get serviced. There is about 14 minutes of wasted time per customer

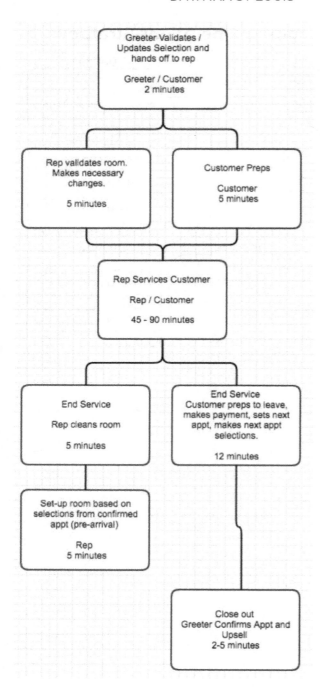

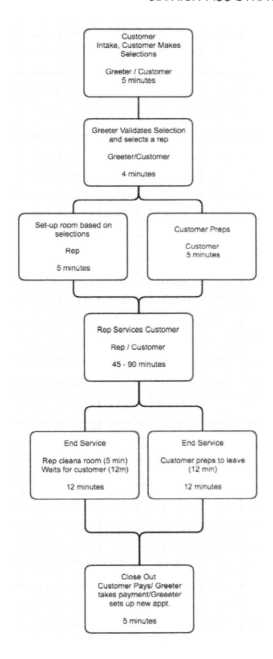

FUTURE STRATEGY

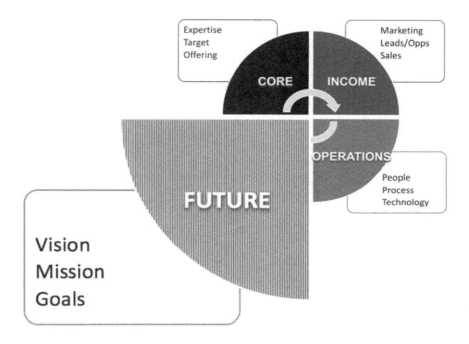

When developing your own Vision Statement (note the word statement and not paragraph) make sure that it answers the question - What does your company want to be in the future? Pick one thing and use that as your guiding force in business.

Your mission statement answers the question – What do you need to do to reach your vision? And your goals are the high-level milestones that you need to reach to accomplish your mission and achieve your vision.

Define Your Vision

Vision Statement: What does your organization want to be or do for their customers? If your company was a child the question would be "What do you want to be when you grow up?" Answer that question for your company.

Define Your Mission

Mission Statement: What does your company need to do to reach your vision?

Define Your Goals

Goals: What actions do you need to take to achieve your mission? Consider goals for the next year or two or five.

Sample Diagram: Future Strategy

VISION

TO BE
The holistic and healthy source of relief, relaxation, and solice for chronic pain sufferers

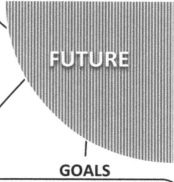

FUTURE

MISSION

TO
Create a sactuary for our customers to be pampered into painless serentiy.

GOALS

TO ACHIEVE
-Top status as the holistic alternative to opioid medications in the medical community
-Three-peat for Best in Service
-Top 20 company to work for on Fortune 500 list

THE DAILY SIX

The Daily 6ix

You have planted the seeds of your business, now it is time to grow it on purpose. The Daily 6ix is where you provide the water, light, and fertilizer to purposely grow your business every day.

You will complete the 2 income production, relationship building, and professional development tasks that you planned the night before. No task will be greater than 48 minutes. Every task will have a goal. When the goal or time is reached, your task is done and you take a break for 12 minutes.

Whatever you don't complete moves to the next day. Take note of the types of tasks that you delay as this may be a point of concern.

DATE _____/_____/_____

INCOME PRODUCTION

Milestone: _____

Actions: _____

_____

Notes:

INCOME PRODUCTION

Milestone: _____

Actions: _____

_____

Notes:

RELATIONSHIP BUILDING

Milestone: _____

Actions: _____

_____

Notes:

RELATIONSHIP BUILDING

Milestone: _____

Actions: _____

_____

Notes:

PROFESSIONAL DEVELOPMENT

Milestone: _____

Actions: _____

_____

Notes:

PROFESSIONAL DEVELOPMENT

Milestone: _____

Actions: _____

_____

Notes:

DATE _____ / _____ / _____

INCOME PRODUCTION

Milestone: _____

Actions: _____

Notes:

INCOME PRODUCTION

Milestone: _____

Actions: _____

Notes:

RELATIONSHIP BUILDING

Milestone: _____

Actions: _____

_____

Notes:

RELATIONSHIP BUILDING

Milestone: _____

Actions: _____

_____

Notes:

PROFESSIONAL DEVELOPMENT

Milestone: _____

Actions: _____

_____

Notes:

PROFESSIONAL DEVELOPMENT

Milestone: _____

Actions: _____

_____

Notes:

DATE _____ / _____ / _____

INCOME PRODUCTION

Milestone: _____

Actions: _____

_____

Notes:

INCOME PRODUCTION

Milestone: _____

Actions: _____

_____

Notes:

RELATIONSHIP BUILDING

Milestone: _____

Actions: _____

_____

Notes:

RELATIONSHIP BUILDING

Milestone: _____

Actions: _____

_____

Notes:

PROFESSIONAL DEVELOPMENT

Milestone: _____

Actions: _____

_____

Notes:

PROFESSIONAL DEVELOPMENT

Milestone: _____

Actions: _____

_____

Notes:

DATE _____ / _____ / _____

INCOME PRODUCTION

Milestone: _____

Actions: _____

_____

Notes:

INCOME PRODUCTION

Milestone: _____

Actions: _____

_____

Notes:

RELATIONSHIP BUILDING

Milestone: _____

Actions: _____

_____

Notes:

RELATIONSHIP BUILDING

Milestone: _____

Actions: _____

_____

Notes:

PROFESSIONAL DEVELOPMENT

Milestone: _____

Actions: _____

_____

Notes:

PROFESSIONAL DEVELOPMENT

Milestone: _____

Actions: _____

_____

Notes:

DATE _____ / _____ / _____

INCOME PRODUCTION

☐ **Milestone:** _____

Actions: _____

_____

Notes:

INCOME PRODUCTION

☐ **Milestone:** _____

Actions: _____

_____

Notes:

RELATIONSHIP BUILDING

Milestone: _____

Actions: _____

_____

Notes:

RELATIONSHIP BUILDING

Milestone: _____

Actions: _____

_____

Notes:

PROFESSIONAL DEVELOPMENT

Milestone: _____

Actions: _____

_____

Notes:

PROFESSIONAL DEVELOPMENT

Milestone: _____

Actions: _____

_____

Notes:

DATE _____ / _____ / _____

INCOME PRODUCTION

Milestone: _____

Actions: _____

_____

Notes:

INCOME PRODUCTION

Milestone: _____

Actions: _____

_____

Notes:

RELATIONSHIP BUILDING

Milestone: _____

Actions: _____

_____

Notes:

RELATIONSHIP BUILDING

Milestone: _____

Actions: _____

_____

Notes:

PROFESSIONAL DEVELOPMENT

Milestone: _____

Actions: _____

_____

Notes:

PROFESSIONAL DEVELOPMENT

Milestone: _____

Actions: _____

_____

Notes:

DATE _____ / _____ / _____

INCOME PRODUCTION

Milestone: _____

Actions: _____

_____

Notes:

INCOME PRODUCTION

Milestone: _____

Actions: _____

_____

Notes:

RELATIONSHIP BUILDING

Milestone: _____

Actions: _____

_____

Notes:

RELATIONSHIP BUILDING

Milestone: _____

Actions: _____

_____

Notes:

PROFESSIONAL DEVELOPMENT

Milestone: _____

Actions: _____

_____

Notes:

PROFESSIONAL DEVELOPMENT

Milestone: _____

Actions: _____

_____

Notes:

ABOUT THE AUTHOR

Like you, serial entrepreneur, Dawnna St Louis has come up with some wickedly amazing ideas. And just like you she knows that turning that idea into profits can feel like running the gauntlet on American Ninja Warrior - over hot coals - in hurricane force winds!

OUCH!

But then things changed. Within three years of starting her business intelligence consultancy, Dawnna developed the 6ix Kick-A$$ Strategies - a radically simple to use business building strategy that transformed a single opportunity into a 9-figure business. After sharing the strategies with her colleagues, she tailored her secret sauce to work for business owners from every walk of life.

Today, Dawnna is the forward-thinking, game-changing, entrepreneur-loving founder of the E-Suite Network – http://www.ESuiteNetwork.com - dedicated to bridging the gap between the 99% and the 1% by educating and coaching ten thousand entrepreneurs into multi-million-dollar business owners.

Her unique blend of edgy humor and deep business knowledge makes her a highly sought out international force of nature as a keynote speaker and straight-talking business strategist.